Date Due

AN 16 1978			

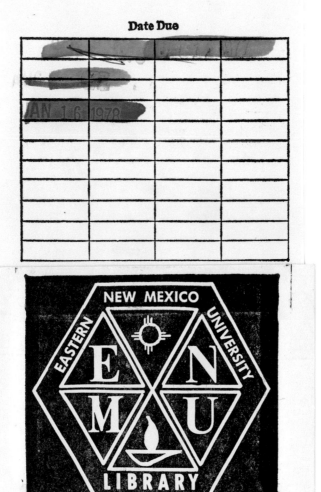

DARK NEBULAE,
GLOBULES,
AND
PROTOSTARS

DARK NEBULAE, GLOBULES, AND PROTOSTARS

BEVERLY T. LYNDS, editor

THE
UNIVERSITY OF ARIZONA
PRESS
Tucson, Arizona

Developed from presentations at the
Symposium on
DARK NEBULAE, GLOBULES, AND PROTOSTARS
March 26, 27, 1970
The University of Arizona
Tucson, Arizona

This publication has been subsidized in part by
The National Science Foundation, Sponsor's Grant No. GP-15266.

THE UNIVERSITY OF ARIZONA PRESS

I.S.B.N.-0-8165-0300-1
L.C. No. 73-152040

A Dedicatory Tribute
to a
Great Scientist
by Jesse L. Greenstein
Hale Observatories

BART JAN BOK

For my scientific lifetime, Bart Bok has been a leader in statistical methods of study of galactic structure and interstellar matter. A few incursions into astrophysics, a permanent love affair with the Carina region (from 1930 to 1970!), and his long-lasting habits of teaching and leadership have prompted this Symposium on Dark Nebulae, Globules, and Protostars. I have known Bart since he arrived at Harvard in 1929, and he was my thesis adviser in 1935–37. At the age of 64 years, he has decided to retire early from the directorship of Steward Observatory, presumably to channel his energy even more efficiently into work on his loved Milky Way.

Bart Jan Bok was born in Hoorn, The Netherlands, in 1906; he studied at Leiden during 1924–27, and at Groningen, 1927–29. He came to the United States and to Harvard University in 1929, married American astronomer Priscilla Fairfield, and was naturalized in 1938. He held the Agassiz and Wilson fellowships, became assistant professor in 1933, associate professor in 1939, and Wheeler professor in 1946, serving for a time as associate director of Harvard Observatory. He became professor and department head at the Australian National University in 1957, and also director of the Mount Stromlo Observatory. He returned to the United States to head the department of astronomy at the University of Arizona in 1966, becoming at the same time director of the Steward Observatory; he supervised the construction of the 90-inch reflector.

He received honors from his native country — the Oranje-Nassau medal and membership in the Royal Netherlands Academy. He is a member of the U. S. National Academy of Sciences, has been commission president in the International Astronomical Union, and serves as vice-chairman of the U. S. National Committee for the IAU. His energy and organizing ability were clearly revealed again recently, when he handled with delicacy the election of new members — an abrasive experience which I trust he has survived in his usual good spirits.

Bok's career in science has influenced all of the fields to which we have directed our attention in this instance. I will try to describe his general scientific style, one that is very much his own, not only representing a link with the great Dutch tradition of statistical astronomy but also leading to work in quite modern fields. Much current research that seems without past roots does in fact depend on the basic picture of our galaxy derived by Kapteyn, Van Rhijn, Seares, and Bok and his students. Statistical parallaxes are still the basis for our distance estimates for various groups of stars. Star counts, first for all stars and later by finer subdivisions, give us the grand picture of the galaxy and supply rough indications of density fluctuations for the interstellar dust and for the stars.

Bok's *The Distribution of the Stars in Space* represents the state of knowledge in 1937, before the development of successful techniques for measurement of the interstellar absorption, and before galactic rotation had been fully integrated with other aspects of galactic structure. It is a characteristic of Bok's style to avoid excessive mathematical detail. The problem of obtaining the space density of stars from the run of the counted number with magnitude is one of inversion of a set of integral equations (Kapteyn 1918) by using a finite number of discrete shells, a trial-and-error method that gives ρ (r), the density, from N (m) and (m, log r) tables. The spread within the luminosity function ϕ (M) makes a mathematical inversion useless, or deceptive.

A number of Bok's pupils counted millions of stars, made (m, log r) tables, and obtained ρ (r) for different parts of the sky. Others determined the effects of dark nebulae, or varying amounts of interstellar absorption on N (m). Both of these results could be obtained analytically, and much had been done before Bok's star-counting brigade started. However, the sensitivity of the results to errors in ϕ (M) or in the absorption was not fully realized until the experience at Harvard. Errors in photometry plagued the Selected Area counts, and only photoelectric techniques — ten years later — made determination of accurate magnitudes and colors possible.

The structure of the galaxy determined this way clearly revealed the density decrease with z-coordinate, but indicated a locally concentrated system, with steep density gradients in the plane, beginning at 0.5 kpc, if the absorption was taken as constant. Detailed knowledge of the absorption as a function of the distance and direction is needed to disentangle stellar density gradients from those in the dust. The spiral arms are concentrations both of bright stars and of dust. The luminosity function depends on position, since stars of high luminosity have such short nuclear lifetimes that they are not found outside the arms. All these complications are mentioned in *The Distribution of the Stars in Space,* in 1937. My own thesis was written on observations and theory of the ratio of absorption to reddening.

Another early interest, which Bok has continued as an active area, is that of the detailed structure of the southern Milky Way. The spiral arm that includes the brilliant and fascinating objects in Carina was the subject of a review by Bok at Basel in 1969. Bok, Hine, and Miller note that Bok in his thesis (1932) was interested in some astrophysical and structural properties of the Cɛ ʾna region. It was the subject of more work in 1937 and 1956; in his Basel Symposium review there are about 70 references, including several to Bok and Bok! It seems clear that the Carina feature is a major center for active star formation, which can be studied now by 21-cm techniques, H II regions, OB stars with UBV photometry, and astrophysically, by individually interesting stars. For example, η Car itself, a slow supernova-like variable had a brighter parallel in the supernova 1961e in NGC 1058. One further important feature of Bok's style is a bulldog determination to get the answer, eventually, if necessary by urging the invention and use of new techniques, and certainly using a lot of bright young men.

Another early subject, still of continuing interest, is the study of the stability of moving clusters (Bok 1934), which Jeans (1922) had studied in an older model of the galaxy. A lower mean density and the existence of a galactic center had to be incorporated in Bok's analysis. This was, in fact, one of Bok's most mathematical papers; it is based on Picart (1892) as described by Tisserand (1896). Globular clusters have been stable since the origin of the galaxy, but Bok noted that while dense galactic clusters were also stable, for 3 x 10^9 years, extended moving clusters were not. Since stability depends on the cluster density as compared to its background, disintegration proceeds by slow expansion due to encounters and shear, followed by a rapid decay. Extended streams would not be stable, and the existence of local streamings was noted with some concern. In fact, Bok predicted that the streams will disintegrate in a modest fraction of the age of the galaxy. Thus, as early as 1934, there was a feeling that perhaps some features of our galaxy were relatively young — without regard to the theory of nuclear energy sources, or to theories of stellar evolution, which later proved that stars are being born.

The rarity of old galactic clusters like M67 and NGC 188 points to the correctness and current interest of this subject. Other researchers (Spitzer, Schwarzschild, King) studied the evaporation rates for stars of different masses, which provide an important new phenomenon — the collapse of the core of a cluster as the less-massive members escape. This suggestion has led to a theory of the explosions in galactic nuclei (Lynden-Bell and others) which provides for runaway phenomena at the centers of dense clusters of stars; these may lead to collapse, implosion and explosion of very massive bodies. Only this suggestion, so far, counterbalances the romantic suggestions (Ambarzumian, Burbidge) of purely explosive events of unknown origin in galactic nuclei.

One last backward glance to the 1930s: One question Shapley asked me, as a student, was how neutral hydrogen in the galaxy could be detected. With infallible predictive skill I said it couldn't be done — since the Lyman lines were in the unobservable ultraviolet, and since the metastability of the 2s level was insufficient to produce observable lines. The discovery of the 21-cm line by Ewen and Purcell (1951) resulted in Harvard, with Bok and pupils, becoming very active in this field; the 21-cm line gave both the velocity and amount of the neutral hydrogen clouds in the galaxy. Since H I is the dominant form of H in the galaxy, and since the abundance of H is 5×10^5 times that of Ca II (producing the interstellar K line) and more than 10^6 times Na I (producing interstellar D lines), what suddenly became clarified was that there was another major constituent of interstellar gas, material out of which the stars are still being born.

Others will discuss the process of star formation, the globules of dust, and the condensations of gas, molecules, and dust about new and old infrared stars. But that entire area also involved Bok as a pioneer, beginning in 1946 when he worked with Miss Reilly on the dark globules. Using work on the nature of the dust by Schalén, and by Greenstein, he estimated minimum masses, the effect of radiation pressure, the velocity of collapse, and suggested that dense globules were protostars. At the same time, Joy, Greenstein, and Herbig had begun to study the spectra of the strange T Tauri variables involved in dense dust clouds, and found evidence of new, strange phenomena, like those of an enormously enhanced unstable solar chromosphere. The entire subject of formation of stars, at a rate needed to balance the deaths of stars and of clusters, was now opened.

I dare not begin to list all the areas of work of our hero, or all of the many students he has inspired; the journals are filled with their papers. I also am not detailing Bok's practical leadership involved with the directorships of Mount Stromlo and of the Steward Observatory. Further, I am but mentioning his devotion to popular education, to lucid articles in popular and semipopular journals, to review and résumé articles, and to international goodwill. The amount I have omitted is far greater than the few specifics I have covered. I have even made what for Bok is the unforgivable omission, I haven't even mentioned the Magellanic Clouds! But I have seen Bok, and I have not seen the Magellanic Clouds. I prefer the mystery and beauty seen to that unknown.

CONTENTS

1. Star Counts and Galactic Structure

S. W. McCUSKEY

Warner and Swasey Observatory, Case Western Reserve University

The use of star counts to delineate the spatial arrangement of the stars in the neighborhood of the sun dates from the time of Sir William Herschel (1784, 1785). Nearly a century later, with the advent of comprehensive star catalogues and charts and photometric surveys, counts according to apparent magnitude led to a more detailed knowledge of the stellar universe. In the first quarter of the twentieth century the pioneering efforts by Kapteyn, Van Rhijn, Seares, and others resulted in the Selected Area program and the tabulations to faint magnitude limits for star numbers in these areas. The tables in *Groningen Publications no. 43* (Van Rhijn 1929) and *Mount Wilson Contribution no. 301* (Seares et al. 1925) have provided useful star-count data for many subsequent purposes. References to these important contributions and a comprehensive summary may be found in the monograph, *The Distribution of the Stars in Space* (Bok 1937).

The development of methods for determining the general luminosity function also can be traced to the efforts of the investigators noted above. The crucial part played by this function in calculating the space densities of stellar groups is, of course, well known. Van Rhijn (1936) published a basic general luminosity function which has served adequately for star-count analysis. Some small modifications in it have resulted from more recent studies, but these have been minor (McCuskey 1966; Luyten 1968).

The influence of interstellar absorption, and in particular nearly opaque interstellar clouds, on the surface distribution of stars has been abundantly documented (Bok 1937; Greenstein 1951; Lynds 1968). Long ago Seeliger (see Deutschland 1919) showed that the true space density $D(r)$ of stars at distance r was related to the apparent density $\triangle(r_0)$, calculated without regard to interstellar absorption, at apparent distance r_0 by the equation

$$D(r) = \Delta(r_0)e^{0.6A(r)/mod}[1 + \frac{0.2rA'(r)}{mod}] \tag{1}$$

where $A(r)$ is the absorption in magnitudes between the sun and a star at true distance r; $A'(r)$ is the derivative of $A(r)$ with respect to r; and $r_o = r\,e^{0.2A(r)/mod}$.

Methods for determining the distance, the radial extent, and the absorbing power of a discrete cloud of interstellar dust from star counts have been summarized by Lynds (1968). It has been amply demonstrated by Schalén (1928), Miller (1937 a, b), Greenstein (1937), Malmquist (1943), Velghe (1956), and others that the large dispersion in the *general luminosity function* ($\sim$2.5-3 mag) makes the determination of such a cloud uncertain. If, instead of general star counts one uses stars grouped into rather narrow intervals of spectral type-luminosity class, the uncertainties can be substantially reduced. We shall return to this point later.

During the period 1930–1950 an extensive program of general star counts and ensuing investigations of galactic structure was initiated at the Harvard College Observatory by B. J. Bok and carried out by him, his students, and by colleagues from other institutions. It was apparent that galactic analysis based on data from small areas uniformly but sparsely spread over the sky was not adequate to reveal the complexity of the Milky Way. The techniques for counting and the use of large fields by Bok and his coworkers resulted in a picture of the surface·distribution of stars over major areas of the northern and southern hemispheres. These researches in general reached photographic magnitude limits of 13 to 15.

Figure 1 shows in broad outline the extensiveness of the work done by Bok and his coworkers. The caption for the figure indicates sources of published material from which the boundaries of the fields were taken. Two of the largest surveys should be mentioned in particular. Data were published, together with analysis, in the inaugural papers, *Investigations of Galactic Structure, I. Counts of Stars with Apparent Magnitudes Brighter than 13.5 in the Southern Hemisphere* (Lindsay and Bok 1937); and II. *The Milky Way from Aquila to Cygnus* (Miller 1937a). This collection of general star count material for the stars brighter than $m_{pg} = 15$ is a rich source of information for planning more detailed studies on sections of the Milky Way.

A summary of space density analysis derived from this and other star count data has been given recently by McCuskey (1965). In brief it may be said that very large local fluctuations within one kiloparsec of the sun occur even when the best available estimates for the interstellar absorption are applied in the analysis. The Cygnus region ($l^{II} = 65°-70°$), the Cepheus region ($l^{II} = 100°-104°$), the Perseus region ($l^{II} = 135°-145°$), and the Auriga-Taurus region ($l^{II}\sim185°$) in the northern sky are noteworthy for their complexity. At present, unfortunately, *detailed* general star counts for Milky Way areas in the southern sky are not available.

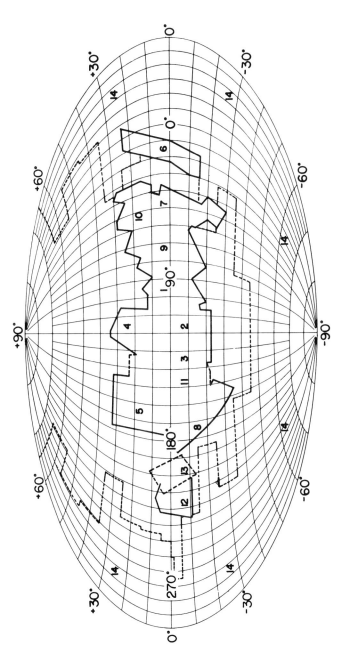

Fig. 1. The sky coverage of the Harvard Star Count Program. Numbers refer to the following sources of data: 1. Risley 1943; 2. Baker 1939; 3. Baker and Nantkes 1944; 4. Nantkes and Baker 1948; 5. Kiefer and Baker 1941; 6. Baker and Kiefer 1942; 7. Baker 1941; 8. McCuskey 1938; 9. Miller 1937a; 10. Calvert 1951; 11. Heeschen 1951; 12. Bok and Rendall-Arons 1945; 13. Bok, Olmsted, and Boutelle 1949; 14. Lindsay and Bok 1937.

A recent contribution by van Hoof (1969), however, may help to fill this gap. Counts were made by van Hoof to $m_{pg} = 16$ on Franklin-Adams plates, which cover approximately 500 square degrees, along the latitude parallel $b^{II} = +21°5$ from $l^{II} = 347°$ to $22°$, and in two fields, for comparison, at $b^{II} = -20°$. Values of log $N(m)$ for $m = 13$, 14, 15, 16 are tabulated for each square degree. This data together with that by Bok (1956), to be discussed later, can contribute to studies of the dark nebulae in Ophiuchus and Scorpius.

The advent of large-field telescopes equipped with objective prisms, and in particular the Schmidt telescope, has made possible the rapid accumulation of spectral-type luminosity-class data for large areas of the sky. Galactic structure analyses therefore can be made for groups of stars in rather narrow intervals of absolute magnitude. For 40 years the Swedish astronomers have been leaders in this type of research, both for the determination of space densities and for the investigation of interstellar absorbing clouds (see, for example, Schalén 1928).

Since 1945 at the Warner and Swasey Observatory we have been studying the local galactic structure by these techniques. Similar studies had already been made by Bok and his coworkers in 1945 (Bok and Rendall-Arons 1945; Bok and Wright 1945). These researches, however, have been limited to rather small areas (~ 20 sq. deg.) of the sky. Therefore, three years ago a large-scale star-count program involving the main sequence A stars and the giant K stars was initiated at the Warner and Swasey Observatory. I would like to report briefly on the current status of this program.

The survey of the galactic belt $b^{II} = 0°$ to $\pm 5°$ for faint ($V \sim 13$ mag) early A stars was undertaken principally for two purposes: (1) to locate real concentrations of these objects which might be connected with the "fossilized" spiral structure of the galaxy in the solar neighborhood; (2) to locate in some detail the regions of space in which the ratio of main sequence A stars to giant stars might give some insight into young versus old groups of A stars which then could be studied profitably by kinematic data.

The objective prism used for this survey, attached to the Burrell Schmidt-telescope, provides a dispersion of 1100 Å/mm at Hγ. On Kodak IIaO plates it is possible to identify with assurance the early A stars brighter than $V = 13$ when an exposure time of 20 minutes is used. Details of the counting process, the counting accuracy, the corrections for plate-to-plate overlap, small corrections to reduce the limiting magnitudes to a reasonably common system, and so on, will be given elsewhere. The limiting magnitudes for the series of plates are determined by comparison with data for galactic clusters. Nancy Houk and I have collaborated on the part of the survey reported here. The final numbers of stars per square degree are the averages, all reductions made independently, for the two investigators.

We report here the results of this A star survey for the galactic belt $l^{II} = 50°$ to $150°$; $b^{II} = 0°$ to $\pm3°$. In a final summary for many parts of this area we shall consider the distribution to $b^{II} = \pm10°$.

Figure 2 presents a comparison of the surface distribution of A stars with the interstellar absorption in the same areas. The upper histogram in each part of the figure for each latitude zone gives N(13), the number of stars brighter than V = 13 per square degree. Each lower histogram shows the interstellar absorption, A_v, at one kiloparsec. For convenience the survey has been divided into three galactic longitude segments: I. Across the local and Perseus spiral arms; II. Along the local spiral arm (or feature) toward Cygnus; III. Between the Cygnus and Sagittarius spiral features. The interstellar absorption has been evaluated from extensive data on color excesses published by Neckel (1967) and by FitzGerald (1968). A ratio $R = A_v/E_{B-V} = 3.1$ has been used to convert color excess into absorption. In each part of Figure 2 the histograms show the departures of the numbers from the averages in each of the three regions. The total number of A stars counted to V = 13, adjusted for overlaps, photometry, and so on, is: Region I, 34,731 in 582 sq. deg.; Region II, 12,153 in 370 sq. deg.; Region III, 8,802 in 382 sq. deg. Thus there is a progressive increase in the average number per square degree from 23.1 in the interarm region (III) to 59.7 in the area which coincides with the broadside local spiral feature.

The majority of the B8–A3 stars are 500 to 1,500 parsecs from the sun, the number brighter than V = 10 being considerably smaller than N(13). Over this entire region the average absorption $<A_v>$ at 500 parsecs is about 1.0–1.2 magnitude, while that at one kiloparsec averages 1.6–2.4 magnitude. The fluctuations from area to area are quite large, however; and it seems clear from a comparison of the histograms in Figure 2 that much of the variation in star numbers is caused directly by the varying absorption. There are, however, exceptional regions in which the values of N(13) indicate excesses or deficiencies which appear to be real. Figure 2 serves as a planning chart to pick out these areas for more detailed study. For illustration, the region in Cepheus, $l^{II} = 100°-105°$, is such a concentration, which we shall examine in more detail.

As a part of the Harvard star count program under the direction of B. J. Bok, general star counts for $m_{pg} \leq 15$ in an area of about 750 square degrees were made by Miss A. M. Risley (1943). A more detailed analysis for the brighter area based on spectral classes was also published by her for an 80 square degree region (Risley 1949). In these studies the interstellar absorption over broad areas, and the space density of stars in smaller sub-areas, were evaluated. These were selected by inspection

6

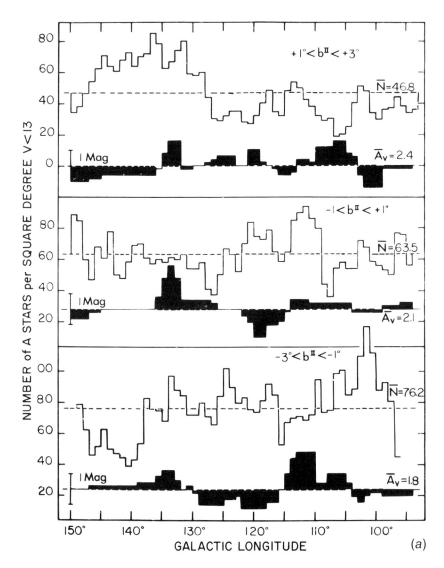

Fig. 2. Surface distribution of B8–A3 stars (V ⩽ 13) and interstellar absorption. (a) $l^{II} = 95°$ to $150°$; (b) $l^{II} = 50°$ to $95°$. Each upper histogram represents variations from the average for 13th magni-

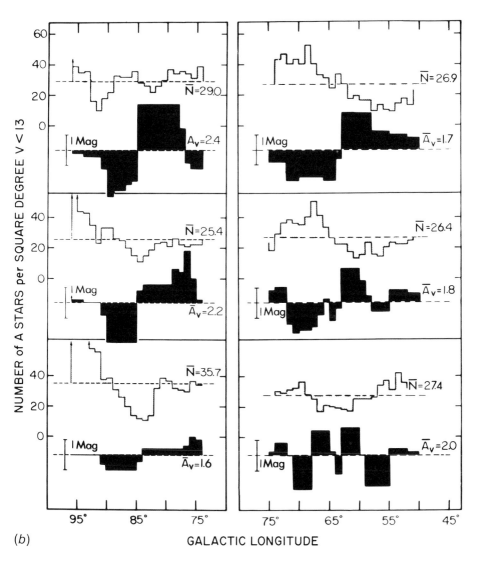

(b)

GALACTIC LONGITUDE

tude star counts; each lower histogram represents the fluctuations in A_V at one kiloparsec relative to the average over the longitude ranges indicated.

of the plates as representing areas of approximately constant surface density of stars. The entire region is included between $85° < l^{II} < 122°$, $-20° < b^{II} < +20°$ but the data do not cover this entire area. Our data for the B8–A3 stars embrace primarily the areas E_1, E_2, E_3, H_1, A, D, J, K, M (Risley 1943, Fig. 1) studied by general star counts. Parts of this region have also been studied by Schalén (1928) and by Wernberg (1941).

A mosaic photograph of the region, made from the National Geographic-Palomar survey prints, together with a galactic coordinate grid, is shown in Figure 3. In Figure 4a are displayed the counted numbers of A stars, $N(13)$ and $N(10)$, in each square degree; in Figure 4b the interstellar absorption, A_v, at 500 and 1,000 parsecs is exhibited. This has been determined from photoelectric color excess data as mentioned above.

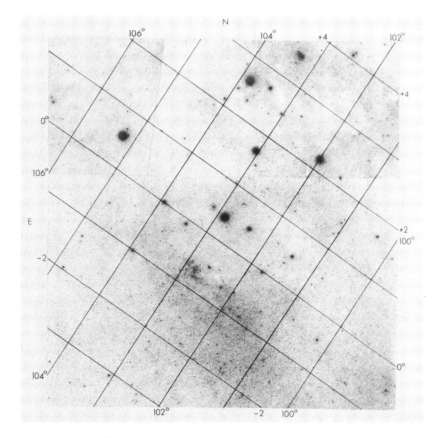

Fig. 3. The complex region in Cepheus.

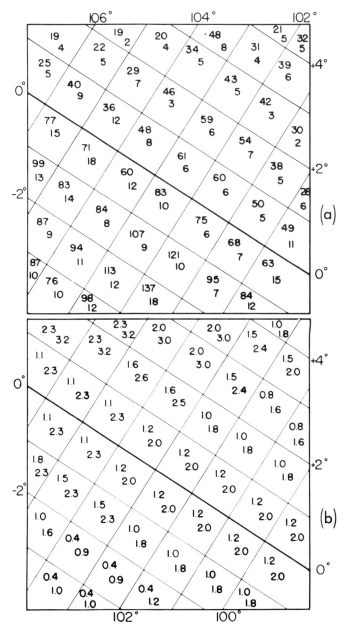

Fig. 4. (a) Star counts for the Cepheus complex (B8–A3 Stars). The upper number in each square degree gives N(13); the lower gives N(10), for the area shown in Figure 3. (b) Interstellar absorption in Cepheus. The upper number in each square is A_V at 0.5 kpc., the lower number is A_V at 1 kpc., for the area shown in Figure 3.

Figures 3 and 4a reveal clearly the complexity of this region as indicated by the surface distribution of the stars. The average of N(13) is 66; that of N(10) is 8.8 over a 56 square degree area. One can show by simple statistical tests that the probability of such a complex pattern arising by random fluctuations is very small. Furthermore there is a strong trend toward increasing surface density with decreasing galactic latitude. In some latitude zones the numbers N(13) may fluctuate by as much as a factor of two even in the limited longitude range shown here. To illustrate that a large part of the observed variation in stellar surface density is due to variations in the absorption, we show in Figure 5a the average log N(13) and average log N(10) for each galactic latitude strip as functions of b^{II}. Vertical bars indicate the ranges in log N(V) entering each average. In Figure 5b are shown the runs of $<A_v>$ at 500 and 1,000 parsecs with galactic latitude. For comparative purposes Figure 5c indicates the trends in $<\log N(m)>$ for $m_{pg} = 11$, 13 and 15 for the general star count data published by Risley (1943).

For either the B8–A3 star counts, or the general star count data, the change in $<\log N>$ over the range $-4° < b^{II} < +4°$ is about 0.5. Also for either set of data $\triangle<\log N>/\triangle m$ is 0.3. Hence to eliminate the observed difference in $<\log N>$ over this latitude range by assigning its cause to variation in A_v would require a $\triangle A_v$ about 1.6. Actually it is evident from Figure 5b that $\triangle A_v$ for $-4° < b^{II} < +4°$ is about 1.1 magnitudes at either 500 or 1,000 parsecs. Within the uncertainties in the data, and the averaging involved, it appears that the major part of the average variation with latitude in the star count data arises from variations that occur in A_v.

Figure 6 illustrates what can be done in the way of a more detailed analysis of the A star counts in three strips of galactic longitude over the range $-5° < b^{II} < +5°$. The variations of log N(13) and log N(10), of A_v at 250, 500, 1,000 and 2,000 parsecs, and of the stellar space density at r = 250, 500, 750, and 1,000 parsecs are shown. For the latter it has been assumed that $M_0 = +0.9$ and $\sigma_0 = 0.7$ for the B8–A3 stars per unit volume of space. The space densities have been corrected for interstellar absorption by the Seeliger formula (Eq. 1). Clearly, with the exceptions of the localized high space density at $b^{II} < 0°$, $l^{II} = 101° - 102°$, and the nearby high density region at $-2° < b^{II} < -1°$, $103° < l^{II} < 104°$, there are no significant differences in the stellar population relative to the galactic plane in this longitude range.

The bright star cloud at $l^{II} = 100° - 102°$, $b^{II} = -2°$ to $-3°$ has been analyzed in detail by Risley (1949), who used spectral type data from the McCormick Observatory. This high density region is included also in LF4, a region investigated by McCuskey (1951) at the Warner and

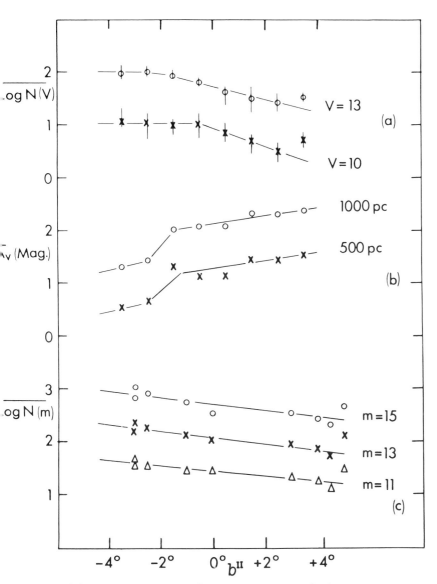

Fig. 5. (a) Averages, $<\log N(13)>$ and $<\log N(10)>$, for galactic latitude zones in the Cepheus complex. Vertical bars indicate the ranges in log N(V) in the averages. (b) The variation of average absorption, $<A_v>$, with galactic latitude. The trends for 0.5 and 1.0 kiloparsec are shown. (c) The trends in $<\log N(m)>$ for general star counts in Cepheus. The data used here are those published by Risley (1943). Curves for m = 11, 13 and 15 are shown.

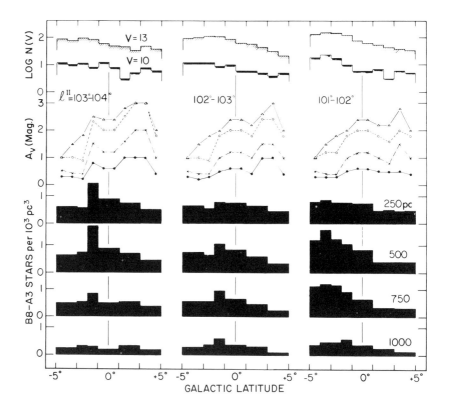

Fig. 6. A detailed analysis of part of the Cepheus complex. At the top are shown the runs of logN(10) and logN(13) with galactic latitude; in the middle are the variations in A_V; below are the variations in space density, stars per 10^3 pc³, for the B8-A3 stars at distances from 250 to 1,000 parsecs.

Swasey Observatory. Both studies confirm the presence of a concentration of A stars between 250 and 750 parsecs from the sun in this direction. The space density in the concentration is 1.5 to 2.5 times that near the sun, or in adjoining ranges in galactic longitude.

Star count methods for determining the distance, radial extent, and total absorption of a cloud of interstellar matter have been fully discussed by Pannekoek (1921), Schalén (1928), Miller (1937a, b), Malmquist (1939, 1943, 1945) and others. Bok (1937) and Lynds (1968) have summarized these. More detailed information concerning the methodology is contained in *Statistical Astronomy* (Trumpler and Weaver 1953). The basic assumptions are: (1) the real distribution of stars in space in the obscured region is the same as that in a nearby apparently unobscured region; (2) if the latter is affected by interstellar absorption of a general nature, the obscured region is affected by the same absorption superimposed on the obscuration by the cloud; (3) the cloud absorption over the observed region is uniform; (4) the distribution of absolute magnitudes of the stars in the two regions is the same and is known. In general it is clear that a meaningful analysis requires areas of the sky which are large enough and contain enough stars to provide statistical strength.

By means of general star counts to faint magnitude limits, very heavily obscured regions may be analyzed to determine total cloud absorptions. Among the many such investigations, we mention here only that by Bok (1956) for the dark nebulae near ρ Ophiuchi and in Taurus. Palomar-Schmidt plates were used for the counts. By comparison of the actual counted numbers with the standard tables by Van Rhijn (1929), Bok was able to show that an obscuration of 7–8 magnitudes in photographic light takes place in the nebula near ρ Ophiuchi; in Taurus the absorption reaches 6 magnitudes in spots. Models of these nebulae were constructed to yield some estimates of density for the interstellar dust. For the nebula near ρ Ophiuchi the central density was estimated to be 0.2 solar masses per cubic parsec. Most of the interstellar grains were found to be confined within a distance of 5 parsecs from the center of the dark cloud. And the total mass of matter within this volume is 27 M$\odot$. The Taurus dark cloud is somewhat more irregular. Here the core area was found to have a total mass of 3 to 5M$\odot$. The large dispersion in absolute magnitude for stars of the general field prohibits any reasonably accurate estimate of the distance of these clouds. The total absorptions, however, can be considered reasonably accurate, since by using faint stars one is relatively sure that the cloud has been completely penetrated.

The effect of the presence of obscuring clouds on general star counts has been considered in considerable detail by Greenstein (1937), by Miller (1937a, b), and others. Since the general stellar luminosity function has a dispersion of something like 2.5–3 magnitudes, these investigators have shown that the use of Wolf diagrams to determine the radial extent and the distance of a cloud leads to elongated cigar-like structures which have little likelihood of being real.

To minimize these difficulties, counts of stars in small intervals of spectral-luminosity class have been used. The Swedish astronomers have been pioneers in these researches; the work by Schalén (1928), Wernberg (1941), Malmquist (1939, 1943, 1945), among others should be mentioned. Malmquist (1943) in particular has indicated how the dispersion in absolute magnitude can influence the dimensions and distance of a nebula. Figure 7 shows an example by Malmquist of the effect of the dispersion on the dimensions of two hypothetical nebulae: (a) a nebula extending from 200 to 400 parsecs absorbing 1.5 magnitudes; (b) a screen at $r = 200$ parsecs absorbing 1.5 magnitudes. This analysis has been made by the use of Wolf diagrams. It is clear that both the initial onset and the radial extent of the cloud are seriously modified as the dispersion increases.

Many of these uncertainties can be removed by analyses based upon the $(m, \log \pi)$ method described by Bok (1937). Here one has the dispersion built into the numerical program. By calculating the run of apparent star density $\triangle(\rho_o)$ with $\rho_o(= 5 \log r_o)$ for both an unobscured (comparison) field and the region of the cloud, one has at hand a systematic way of reconciling the two since it is assumed that the stellar space density *actually* is the same in both. Malmquist (1939) has indicated an easy graphical way to do this. It is based on the principle that the actual number of stars to a true distance r, per unit solid angle, equals the number of stars in the same space cone to an apparent distance $r_o = r \cdot 10^{0.2A(r)}$ computed without regard to absorption. If there is a general, noncloud absorption overlying the regions, this can also be allowed for.

To illustrate this method we use two areas in the Cepheus complex (Fig. 3). Region A at $l^{II} = 101°−103°$, $b^{II} = −3°$ to $−1°$ is considered the clear, or comparison region; region B at $l^{II} = 101°−103°$, $b^{II} = +1°$ to $+3°$ is considered to be obscured by an interstellar cloud. The basic results of the analysis are displayed in Figure 8. In Figure 8, parts *a* and *b* show the differential and the cumulative Wolf curves for the two areas. The ordinates are the logarithms of the number of stars per 100 square degrees and of stars per square degree, respectively, in half magnitude intervals. These have been analyzed by the $(m, \log \pi)$ method with $M_o = 0.9$ $\sigma_o = 0.7$, and also by the Schwarzschild (1912) method programmed for a Univac 1108 computer. The results for the apparent space densities agreed well. In Figure 8(c) we show the resulting runs of $\triangle(\rho_o)$ as functions of $\rho_o(= 5 \log r_o)$, where r_o is the apparent distance in each area.

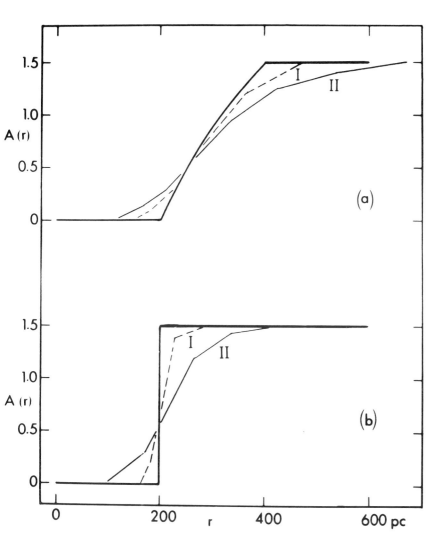

Fig. 7. The effects of dispersion in absolute magnitude on distance and radial extent of obscuring clouds. (a) A cloud extending from 200 to 400 parsecs; (b) a thin screen at 200 parsecs. The heavy lines indicate the run of A(r) for $\sigma = 0$; curves I, for $\sigma = 0.5$; curves II, for $\sigma = 1.0$ mag. dispersion in absolute magnitude.

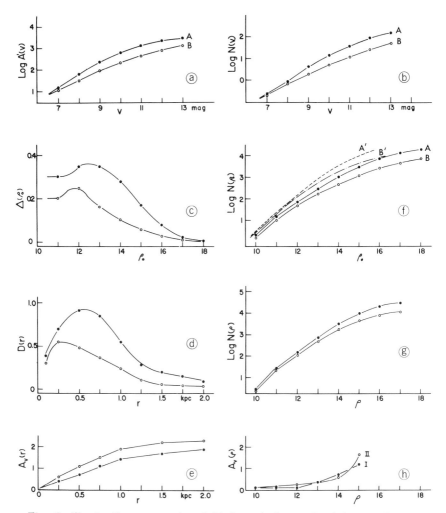

Fig. 8. Illustrative example of Malmquist's method for analysis of an obscuring cloud. See the text for explanation of the parts of the figure. The filled circles refer in each case to the "clear" region; the unfilled refer to the obscured; in part h, curve I results from use of part f, curve II results from part g.

From the analysis of color excess data in these regions the runs of $A_v(r) = 3.1\ E_{B-V}$ with true distance r have been derived. Then the values of $\triangle(\rho_o)$ have been corrected by Seeliger's formula (Eq. 1) to yield the true space density functions, $D(r)$, shown in Figure 8(d). The variation of A_v with distance is displayed in Figure 8(e).

In Figure 8(f) we show: A, the cumulative space density, in logarithmic form, for the clear region; B, that for the obscured region; A' and B', these corrected for absorption according to Figure 8(e). Here $N(\rho_o)$ is the *total* number of stars from the sun to *apparent* distance ρ_o per square degree. For comparative purposes Figure 8(g) indicates the cumulative *true* space densities deduced from Figure 8(d) as functions of ρ, where ρ is the true value 5 log r.

Finally in Figure 8(h) are displayed the curves showing the relative absorption, $A_v(\rho)$, for the obscured region with respect to the clear. Curve I is deduced from Figure 8 (f), A' and B'; curve II is obtained from Figure 8(g).

It is clear from Figures 8(f) and 8(g) that the run of log $N(\rho)$ for the obscured region begins to deviate from that of the clear region at about $\rho = 12.5$. This corresponds to a distance of about 300 parsecs. The extent of the cloud cannot be determined since parallelism of the log $N(\rho)$ curves is not achieved within the limits of the data.

Table 1 summarizes the results for this illustrative example. Columns 2 and 3, respectively, show the trend of the absorption, $A_v(r)$, in the obscured compared to the clear region as evaluated by Malmquist's method using the cumulative star densities shown in Figures 8(f) and 8(g). Columns 4 and 5 show, respectively, the absorption as deduced directly from the cumulative and the differential Wolf diagrams, Figures 8(b) and 8(a). In column 6 the results of an analysis by Wernberg (1941) are displayed for comparison. These refer to his region M3 com-

TABLE 1

Comparative Absorption Values — Cepheus Region

(A_v in mag.)

r(pc)	$\Delta(\rho_o)$ Analysis	D(r) Analysis	Cumulative Wolf Curve	Differential Wolf Curve	Wernberg (1941)
250	0.1	0.25	0.3	0.4	0.3
500	0.5	0.45	0.7	1.0	0.5
750	0.9	0.8	1.1	1.5	0.7
1000	1.2	1.7	1.6	1.9	1.0

pared to his clear region L1. Wernberg's results were derived from cumulative Wolf diagrams for several groups of stars ranging in absolute magnitude from -1.7 to $+2.5$. He used points on the Wolf curves where parallelism first set in as his distance indicators.

The entries in Table 1 give some indication of the accuracy obtainable by such studies. We find $A_v(r)$ increasing markedly in the obscured area at about $r = 300$ pc. Wernberg finds essentially the same onset of the cloud. Whereas we find no indication of a finite cloud thickness from the data at hand, Wernberg concludes that the total absorption in the cloud is 1.1 magnitude. But he also finds from the B7-stars an absorption of 1.8 magnitude, which he ascribes to a distant dark cloud.

It should be apparent that a detailed analysis of such a cloud complex requires data for groups of stars of differing absolute magnitudes but having small dispersions in M_v. The data should extend to faint stars so that total penetration of the obscuring cloud occurs. When data for a single spectral group such as the B8–A3 stars are used there always remains the possibility that a so-called "bright region" is a real concentration of the stars and not simply an area of low obscuration. Let the reader decide, for example, whether the "clear" area in Cepheus used here represents a concentration of A stars or a region of relatively low interstellar absorption compared to the "obscured" area. Certainly the interstellar absorption evaluated from the color excess data is not greatly different in the two regions.

The program of A star counts described here is a part of the continuing research on "Low Dispersion Astronomical Spectroscopy and Galactic Structure" at the Warner and Swasey Observatory supported by the National Science Foundation.

Discussion

H. Weaver: I have one comment: that is, there may be an additional bit of information that can be added in the Cepheus region. As seen in neutral hydrogen, this is a rather extraordinary part of the galaxy in that it shows many fine details. Even without any preconceived ideas about this region, one will immediately stop and search here because the region is full of very small features that do not appear at adjacent longitudes.

REFERENCES

Baker, R. H. 1939, *Harvard Circ.* no. 424.

————. 1941, *Astrophys. J.* 94: 493.

Baker, R. H., and Kiefer, L. 1942, *Astrophys. J.* 96: 224.

Baker, R. H., and Nantkes, E. 1944, *Astrophys. J.* 99: 125.

Bok, B. J. 1937, *The Distribution of the Stars in Space* (Chicago: University of Chicago Press), Chapter 2.

————. 1956, *Astr. J.* 61: 309.

Bok, B. J., Olmsted, M., and Boutelle, B. D. 1949, *Astrophys. J.* 110: 21.

Bok, B. J., and Rendall-Arons, J. M. 1945, *Astrophys. J.* 101: 280.

Bok, B. J., and Wright, F. W. 1945, *Astrophys. J.* 101: 300.

Calvert, R. L. 1951, *Astrophys. J.* 114: 123.

Deutschland, G. 1919, *Vierteljahrschrift Astr. Ges.* 54: 25.

FitzGerald, M. P. 1968, *Astr. J.* 73: 983.

Greenstein, J. L. 1937, *Ann. Harv. Coll. Obs.* 105: 359.

————. 1951, *Astrophysics,* ed. J. A. Hynek (New York: McGraw-Hill Book Co. Inc.), Chapter 13.

Heeschen, D. S. 1951, *Astrophys. J.* 114: 132.

Herschel, W. 1784, *Phil. Trans.* 74: 437.

————. 1785, *Phil. Trans.* 75: 213 (and *Collected Scientific Papers* vol. I. London: 1912; pp. 157 & 223).

Kiefer, L., and Baker, R. H. 1941, *Astrophys. J.* 94: 482.

Lindsay, E. M., and Bok, B. J. 1937, *Ann. Harv. Coll. Obs.* 105: 255.

Luyten, W. J. 1968, *Mon. Not. R. astr. Soc.* 139: 221.

Lynds, B. T. 1968, *Nebulae and Interstellar Matter,* eds. B. M. Middlehurst and L. H. Aller (Chicago: University of Chicago Press), Chapter 3.

McCuskey, S. W. 1938, *Astrophys. J.* 88: 209.

————. 1951, *Astrophys. J.* 113: 672.

————, 1965, *Galactic Structure,* eds. A. Blaauw and M. Schmidt (Chicago: University of Chicago Press), Chapter 1.

————. 1966, *Vistas in Astronomy* 7: 141.

Malmquist, K. G. 1939, *Stockholm Obs. Ann.* 13: no. 4.

————. 1943, *Uppsala astr. Obs. Ann.* 1: no. 7.

————. 1945, *Uppsala astr. Obs. Ann.* 1: no. 8.

Miller, F. D. 1937a, *Ann. Harv. Coll. Obs.* 105: 297.

————. 1937b, *Astr. J.* 46: 165.

Nantkes, E., and Baker, R. H. 1948, *Astrophys. J.* 107: 113.

Neckel, T. 1967, *Veroff. Landessternw. Heidelberg-Königstuhl,* vol. 19.

Pannekoek, A. 1921, *Proc. Kon. Akad. Wetensch. Amsterdam,* 23: no. 5.

Risley, A. M. 1943, *Astrophys. J.* 97: 277.

—————. 1949, *Astrophys. J.* 109: 314.

Schalén, C. 1928, *Uppsala astr. Obs. Medd,* no. 37.

Schwarzschild, K. 1912, *Astr. Nach.* 190: 361.

Seares, F. H., van Rhijn, P. J., Joyner, M. C., and Richmond, M. L. 1925, *Astrophys. J.* 62: 320 (Mount Wilson Contr. 301).

Trumpler, R. J., and Weaver, H. F. 1953, *Statistical Astronomy* (Berkeley: University of California Press [2nd ed.; 1962, New York: Dover Publications]), Chapter 5.

van Hoof, A. 1969, *Bull. astr. Inst. Netherl (Suppl. Ser.)* 3: 137.

van Rhijn, P. J. 1929, *Publ. Kapteyn astr. Lab.* no. 43.

—————. 1936, *Publ. Kapteyn astr. Lab.* no. 47.

Velghe, A. G. 1956, *Astr. J.* 61: 241.

Wernberg, G. 1941, *Uppsala astr. Obs. Ann.* 1: no. 4.

2. A Dark Absorbing Cloud in Carina

J. A. GRAHAM

Cerro Tololo Inter-American Observatory*

The main aim of this contribution is to bring to attention a method that has been used to study the interstellar absorption with considerable success in the past but which also shows great promise for the immediate future as a result of the several new OB star surveys that are now becoming available. The idea is an old one and consists simply of mapping the variations of OB star color excesses across an area of the Milky Way. The method was followed, for example, by Stebbins, Huffer, and Whitford (1939, 1940) who used as their basic data photoelectrically determined colors of 1332 O to B5 stars from the Henry Draper Catalog. One major difficulty with this type of analysis is that there are rarely sufficient numbers of O and B stars known in any one region to make the network of reddening values tight enough to define individual dust clouds. By using the more numerous late B, A, and F-type stars, it is possible to improve the situation, but only over a smaller volume of space at the same apparent magnitude limit.

Strömgren and Crawford (Strömgren 1962) have given some results of such a study. They used U, B, V, and Hβ observations of 501 B8 and B9 stars to derive distance, reddening, and absorption parameters for each star. They were then able to show that the nearby absorption in low galactic latitudes was distributed very irregularly. In some fields there was little absorption, but in others the high absorption values tended to cluster in clouds of diameter approximately 40 parsecs.

I have completed a study of the space distribution of 436 OB-type stars in a field of approximately 50 square degrees in the Carina section of the southern Milky Way. Here, the OB stars are very numerous, and it is possible to treat the absorption data in a way similar to that followed

* Operated by the Association of Universities for Research in Astronomy, Inc., under contract with the National Science Foundation.

by Strömgren and Crawford. The observational data consist of 5-color
and Hβ photometry on the systems of Walraven and Walraven and of
Crawford respectively. The color excesses are determined generally from
the Walraven (V-B) and (B-V) color indices following the procedure
outlined by Morgan and Harris (1956). The observations as well as the
details of the reddening value derivations are given in a recent paper
(Graham 1970).

In this present report, only stars with distance moduli less than 13.0
(distance less than 4 kiloparsecs) are considered. These stars are fairly
evenly distributed over the longitude range of the Carina field. From the
list of stars satisfying this criterion, three groups are formed according
to the color excess E_{V-B}, which is defined as being the difference (V-B)

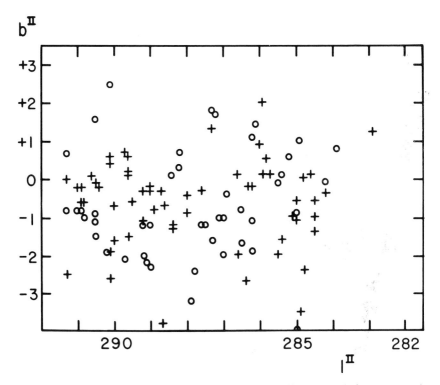

Fig. 1. Galactic latitude and longitude distribution of the group 1
and group 2 stars. Group 1, represented by circles, is made up of
stars with Walraven (V-B) color excesses less than 0.12. Group 2,
represented by crosses, is made up of stars with Walraven (V-B)
color excesses between 0.16 and 0.20.

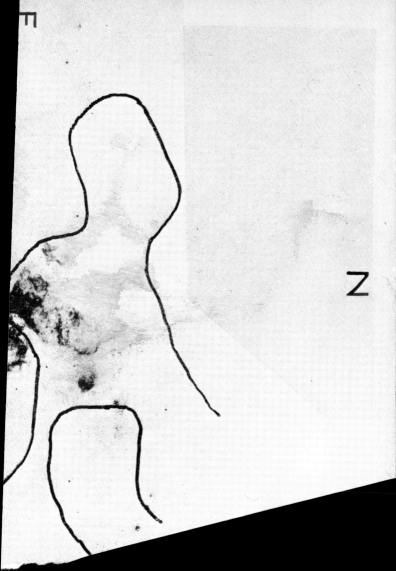

(V-B) intrinsic. Group 1 contains stars with $E_{V-B} < 0.12$; stars with $0.16 < E_{V-B} < 0.20$; and group 3, stars with .25. Note that the Walraven magnitudes and colors are expressed ositive logarithmic scale with base 10. A rough conversion to ɔ-V) Johnson color excess, E_{B-V}, can be made by multiplying by 2.5.

Figure 1 shows the distribution of the stars in the first two groups. one might expect, the group 2 stars lie systematically closer to the galactic plane than the little-reddened group 1 stars. The reddening of the group 2 stars is apparently rather evenly distributed. However, in Figure 2, the points representing the heavily reddened stars show a rather different distribution. They are found predominantly at longitudes less

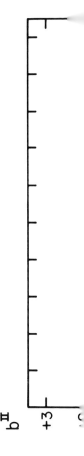

b^{II}

$+3$

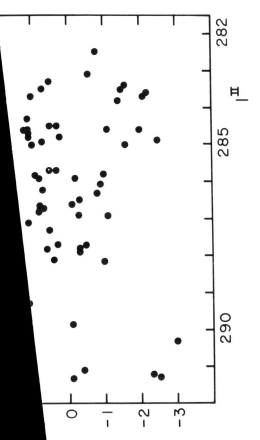

Fig. 2. Galactic latitude and longitude distribution of the group 3 stars. Group 3 contains stars with Walraven (V-B) color excesses greater than 0.25.

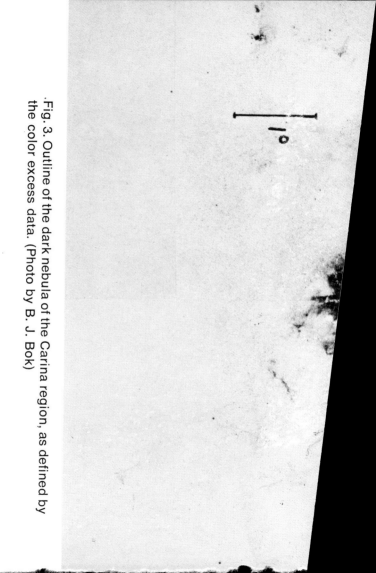

Fig. 3. Outline of the dark nebula of the Carina region, as defined by the color excess data. (Photo by B. J. Bok)

than 287°. It seems that here we are observing a discrete absorbing cloud which is outlined by the distribution of the stars with high color excesses. I have attempted to show this in Figure 3, which was taken from a mosaic photograph kindly provided by B. J. Bok.

At this stage, I should mention that none of this is really new. The dark nebula that I have outlined can be seen clearly with a pair of binoculars on a dark night from Cerro Tololo Observatory, silhouetted against the bright Milky Way. Part of the nebula was discussed by Bok in his thesis (Bok 1932). The new observations just tell us a little more about it. It is probably well on this side of the great Carina Nebula, which it partially obscures. Several sources (see, for example: Sher 1965; Feinstein 1969) show that the distance of the η Carina complex is probably between 2.5 and 3.0 kiloparsecs. However, many of the reddened stars behind the absorbing cloud have distances less than 1.5 kiloparsecs. Few OB stars are known within one kiloparsec of the sun in this direction, and the fact that only isolated unreddened OB stars are seen in front of the cloud suggests that it is probably closer than one kiloparsec. The present observations are consistent with the distance 0.8 kiloparsec given by Bok. Remembering that at 0.8 kiloparsec $1° = 15$ parsecs, we see that the dimensions of the cloud are in the 20 to 50 parsec range.

The average reddening of the 62 stars behind the dark nebula is 0.244 units in (V-B). Just outside the nebula the average for 138 stars is 0.158 units. The difference of 0.086 units corresponds to a Johnson E_{B-V} color excess of 0.22 magnitudes. The total visual and photographic absorption is not high. In the section studied by Bok, 0.8 magnitudes of photographic absorption was found. Although an accurate determination is not possible, it does seem unlikely that a ratio of total visual to selective absorption much higher than 3 can apply to this interstellar dust cloud.

Discussion

H. Weaver: I have one comment about the Carina problem. Here again we find the importance of using the information from stars coupled with the information from interstellar hydrogen, in order to interpret this type of feature. At the present time, for example, there does seem to be a rather large amount of confusion in regard to the interpretation of the hydrogen picture in that particular direction in Carina, and I think that the key to that problem will come through the work that Graham has been doing. His recent study, with its large amount of observational material, will to a large extent solve the problem of the confusion of the structure as seen in hydrogen in that direction. It does seem that perhaps the unification of all of the various techniques and methods, in which Bok has been a prolific practitioner, is the way to follow such problems.

REFERENCES

Bok, B. J. 1932, *Harvard Reprints Series* I, no. 77.
Feinstein, A. 1969, *Monthly Notices Roy. Astron. Soc.* 143: 273.
Graham, J. A. 1970, *Astron. J.* 75: 703.
Morgan, W. W., and Harris, D. L. 1956, *Vistas in Astronomy,* vol. 2, edited by A. Beer (Pergamon Press, London and N.Y.) p. 1124.
Sher, D. 1965, *Quarterly Journal Roy. Astron. Soc.* 6: 299.
Stebbins, J., Huffer, C. M., and Whitford, A. E. 1939, *Astrophys. J.* 90: 209.
———. 1940, *Astrophys. J.* 91: 20.
Strömgren, B. 1962, *The Distribution and Motion of Interstellar Matter in Galaxies,* ed. L. Woltjer (W. A. Benjamin, Inc., New York) p. 38.

3. Note on Accurate Color Excess

D. L. CRAWFORD

*Kitt Peak National Observatory**

Accurate determination of color excesses is necessary for a detailed study of interstellar absorption, whether over the sky or within local regions such as clusters or associations. If excesses are accurate enough, even clouds causing quite small absorption should be detectable.

As early B-type stars are intrinsically bright, they can be used as probes of absorption to distances of several kiloparsecs, but such stars are relatively rare in space. Late B-type stars are more useful as probes for detailed areal studies, as their space density is higher. A- and F-type stars enable the net to be tightened considerably, but they are not observable to distances as far as the B stars. Of course, one should choose the type stars most useful for the program in mind. B-types are especially useful for general features of absorption on a large scale, and F-types for detailed study of nearby clouds, for example.

I would like to mention three techniques that enable one to determine an accurate excess, and to describe one of them, the least used so far, in a little detail. Other techniques exist, of course.

The first technique can be used for stars of all spectral types, with varying degrees of accuracy. If one has, or can observe, the MK spectral type and $(B-V)$ or similar color index, then published calibrations of intrinsic colors of that color index in terms of the MK type can be used to obtain the color excess; for example: $E(B-V) = (B-V) - (B-V)_0$. The MK type may also be used to estimate the star's absolute magnitude, and with the de-reddened apparent magnitude, $V_0 = V - 3E(B-V)$, one may then calculate the distance. There are potential problems involving the ratio of total-to-selective absorption and other things that I won't dwell on here.

*Operated by the Association of Universities for Research in Astronomy, Inc., under contract with the National Science Foundation.

The second technique involves UBV data alone, and works well only for B-type stars. One can calculate the intrinsic color by assuming a linear relation between the intrinsic color indices $(U-B)_o$ and $(B-V)_o$ and a slope of the reddening line $E(U-B)/E(B-V)$, which need not be linear. For a reddening slope of 0.72, and $(B-V)_o/(U-B)_o = 0.27$, $(U-B)_o = 1.242(U-B)-0.894(B-V)$. The color excess follows: $E(U-B) = (U-B)-(U-B)_o$. The equation doesn't work for supergiants, but I believe for other B stars it yields more accurate color excess than the first technique.

The third method involves use of the *uvby* intermediate-band system (Strömgren 1966; Crawford 1966, 1970) and the β narrow-band system (Crawford and Mander 1966). For the A stars, $(b-y)_o = 2.943-1.0\beta$ $- 0.1\delta c_1 - 0.1\delta m_1$, where $0.1\delta c_1$ is a correction term for luminosity effects and $0.1\delta m_1$ is a correction term for blanketing effects. I won't go into details of the calibration here, or discuss the situation for the F stars, except to summarize that the derived mean error of the intrinsic color, for one star, is $\pm 0^m011$ for the A stars and $\pm 0^m015$ for the F stars. As the data for metallic line stars, spectroscopic binaries, and so on, are included in the calibration process, I believe that the mean error reflects the true cosmic scatter of the calibration. The details of the calibration are to be published. Table 1 shows the result of calculating an average value of the coefficient A in the equation $(b-y) = A-1.0\beta-0.1\delta c_1-0.1\delta m_1$ for the A-type stars $(2^m880>\beta>2^m700$ and $\delta c_1<0.280)$ and for three open clusters.

Needless to say there are many possible applications of this technique. I'll mention only one. At Kitt Peak and Cerro Tololo we have been observing foreground, A-type, field stars in the areal vicinity of globular clusters in an effort to derive minimum values of interstellar reddening

TABLE 1

Average Values for Coefficient A (see equation below) for A-type Stars

	A	No. of Stars	Mean error (1 star)
Field stars	2.943^m	484	0.011^m
Praesepe	2.942	37	.013
Hyades	2.945	31	.007
Coma	2.940	8	.006

$(b-y) = A - 1.0\beta - 0.1\delta c_1 - 0.1\delta m_1$

TABLE 2

Color Calibrations for B-type Stars

c_o	$(b-y)_o$	$(U-B)_o$	$(B-V)_o$	Sp.
0.00	−0.116	−0.98	−0.24	B1
.20	−0.097	−0.79	−0.20	B2
.40	−0.077	−0.60	−0.16	B5
.60	−0.058	−0.46	−0.125	B8
.80	−0.038	−0.30	−0.09	B9
1.00	−0.019	−0.14	−0.05	(A0)

$(b-y)_o = -0.116 + 0.097c_o$
$E(c_1) = 0.2E(b-y)$
$E(u-b) = 1.7E(b-y)$
$(u-b)_o = 1.14(u-b) - 1.94(b-y) - 0.22$

between us and the cluster. The first publication describing results has appeared (Crawford and Barnes 1969), and the technique seems to be working well.

The preliminary calibration for B-type stars is given in Table 2, along with four equations involved in the procedure. I have also listed the intrinsic colors $(U-B)_o$ and $(B-V)_o$ and the approximate spectral type, for reference. For B stars, c_1 is a good measure of the strength of the Balmer discontinuity, which is a good function of effective temperature and hence intrinsic color. This good functional relationship between the discontinuity and intrinsic color is why the second technique works well, of course. Here, though, an iterative procedure is used: $(b-y)_o' = -0.116+0.097c_1$, thus $E'(b-y) = (b-y)-(b-y)_o'$, and $E(c_1) = 0.2E'(b-y)$; then $c_o = c_1 - E(c_1)$, and $(b-y)_o = -0.116+0.097c_o$. One such iteration is sufficient for excesses less than one magnitude.

One could also use a technique similar to the second; as $E(u-b) = 1.7E(b-y)$, it follows that $(u-b)_o = 1.14 (u-b)-1.94(b-y)-0.22$. Then $E(u-b) = (u-b)-(u-b)_o$. Note that $E(U-B) \simeq E(b-y)$, for $E(U-B) \simeq 0.72E(B-V)$ and $E(b-y) \simeq 0.70E(B-V)$.

We have nearly finished the reductions of our 4-color and Hβ data for stars of spectral types $\leq$B5 and $m_v < 6.5$ for both northern and southern hemispheres. The data for the southern stars of types $\leq$GO and $m_v < 5.0$ are now in press (Crawford, Barnes, Golson 1970). Analysis of this data will enable us to lay out a picture of the interstellar absorption in the solar neighborhood in some detail. Already it appears to me that the B stars in the south have on the average less absorption than those in

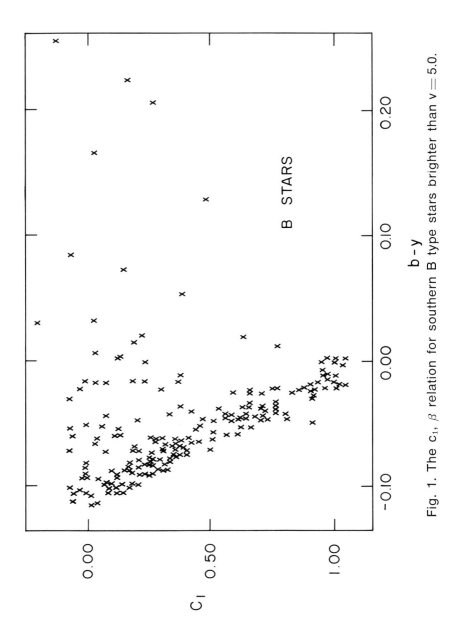

Fig. 1. The c_1, β relation for southern B type stars brighter than v = 5.0.

the north. Figure 1 is a plot of the c_1, (b−y) data for these southern B stars (Sp $\leq$AO, m_v $<$5.0). Little reddening is apparent for most of the stars. As with the A-type stars, numerous applications are apparent to problems of the interstellar absorbing clouds.

Discussion

B. Bok: Would you care to make a comment about the luminosity effects? *Crawford*: We can also calibrate, with considerably more difficulty, absolute magnitudes in terms of these parameters. We find that for the late Bs and early As we seem to be getting a mean error on the order of about 0.3 magnitude. For the early Bs it is more like 0.5 magnitude or even a bit more, because of the nature of the H Beta parameter's variation with absolute magnitude. Distances, of course, are helpful in the laying out of the positions of the dark nebulae.

Bok: And how faint will you be able to go in apparent magnitude? *Crawford:* The faintest stars measured in H Persei were done without real difficulty down to 15th magnitude.

REFERENCES

Crawford, D. L. 1966, *I.A.U. Symp. no. 24,* p. 170.
————. 1970, *I.A.U. Colloq. no. 4,* p. 114.
Crawford, D. L., and Barnes, J. V. 1969, *Astron J.* 74: 1008.
Crawford, D. L., Barnes, J. V., and Golson, J. C. 1970, *Astron J.,* vol. 75 (June).
Crawford, D. L., and Mander, J. 1966, *Astron. J.* 71: 114.
Strömgren, B. 1966, *Ann. Rev. Astronomy and Astrophysics* 4: 433.

4. Globules

BART J. BOK,
CAROLYN S. CORDWELL, AND RICHARD H. CROMWELL
Steward Observatory

More than twenty years ago, Bok and Reilly (1947) and Bok (1948) called attention to the probable importance of dark globules for the study of star birth and evolution. The objects under consideration are roundish, dark nebulae of various dimensions, mostly quite small, which may well be the precursors of protostars. Many of these dark nebulae have diameters as small as 1/25 parsec, less than 10,000 astronomical units; several globules have been found by Thackeray (1964) in IC 2944 with indicated diameters equal to about one quarter of this value. These small globules can be observed only when seen projected against the luminous background of emission nebulae, such as NGC 2244, IC 2944, NGC 3603, and Messier 8. Isolated larger globules are observed all along the band of the Milky Way, especially in regions of dark nebulosity, Taurus and Ophiuchus for example. The radii of the larger globules are in the range 0.1 to 1 parsec; most of these small dark nebulae seem to have no emission or reflection nebulosity associated with them. The largest observed unit dark nebulae have radii as large as 4 parsecs. The dark nebula south of ρ Ophiuchi and some of the nebulae in Taurus and the Southern Coalsack are examples of these large unit clouds. These have been studied in some detail by Bok (1956).

Since distance estimates and minimum total absorptions are obtainable for most globules and dark nebulae, minimum particle masses may be derived. It seems likely that gaseous molecules co-exist with the cosmic grains, either in free form or condensed upon the grain nuclei. Hence the true total masses of the globules and small dark nebulae are probably considerably larger than the derived minimum particle masses; over the years a correction factor of 100 has often been applied to account for the undetected gaseous component. It is most significant that Heiles (1968, 1969) has found OH near the center of the dense dark nebula south of ρ Ophiuchi. The indication is that the temperature is under $10°$ K near the center of this dark nebula. We obviously are gathering some information about the physical conditions inside globules of various dimensions.

It is our aim here to provide a short list of globules representative of various types. Such a list is much needed for use by both optical and radio astronomers. It seems likely that globules and small dark nebulae represent centers of concentration for several varieties of molecules that have been detected in recent years by radio techniques and for molecules yet to be discovered. The radio astronomers obviously need small check lists of representative globules and dark nebulae. Possibilities for optical studies have widened also in recent years. Many large reflectors, several with Ritchie-Chrétien optics, are now in operation, and even larger ones will become available in the course of the next five years. Through the use of image conversion tubes, the sky limit of brightness for direct photography in a wide range of colors can now be reached with exposure times of half an hour and less. A complete study of semi-transparent globules is now a relatively straightforward project, which does not require excessive amounts of large-telescope time.

Table 1 contains a check list of sixteen centers near which one or more good sample globules or dark nebulae are located. All globules in Table 1 are within reach of northern hemisphere telescopes, but six of them are sufficiently far south to be accessible as well to the major southern hemisphere telescopes, optical as well as radio. The dark nebulae south of ρ Ophiuchi and in Taurus may be added to the list; southern hemisphere observers may wish to add to Table 1 the emission nebulae IC 2944, NGC 3576 and NGC 3603, as well as the Southern Coalsack. The 1975 coordinates for these regions are:

Ophiuchus region:	$\alpha = 16^h\,24^m, \delta = -23.4°$
Taurus A:	$\alpha = 4^h\,32^m, \delta = +26.2°$
Taurus B:	$\alpha = 4^h\,38.5^m, \delta = +25°\,39'$
IC 2944:	$\alpha = 11^h\,36.2^m, \delta = -62°\,38'$
NGC 3576:	$\alpha = 11^h\,10.8^m, \delta = -61°\,11'$
NGC 3603:	$\alpha = 11^h\,23.0^m, \delta = -61°\,7'$
Southern Coalsack:	$\alpha = 12^h\,51.5^m, \delta = -63°\,8'$

The source lists from which the globules in Table 1 were selected are Barnard's list (1927) of "dark markings," the Lynds (1962) *Catalogue of Dark Nebulae Found on the Palomar Sky Atlas Charts,* and especially the tabulation of globules published recently by Sim (1968), which lists what are, according to her analysis, 63 certain and 63 probable globules found in regions near OB associations and young star clusters. An early paper by Stoddard (1945) was found useful in the preparation of our list. Reference has also been made to the lists of Schoenberg (1964), Khavtassi (1955), and Roshkovsky (1955). The globules of Table 1, and many others, were inspected on the Palomar prints, and the final sample was selected by Bok and Cordwell as being representative.

Bok (1948) used as a basis for calculations of minimum masses for globules a value,

$$Kpg = 2 \times 10^4, \tag{1}$$

as the most likely value for the amount of photographic extinction in magnitudes produced by one gram of cosmic dust distributed over a column with a base of 1 cm². Spitzer (1968) has suggested a slightly higher value based on van de Hulst's calculations (van de Hulst 1949), and it seems reasonable to use it instead of the earlier value. Hence:

$$Kpg = 4.5 \times 10^4. \tag{2}$$

If the column has a height D (parsecs) and if the density of the cosmic dust in grams per cm³ equals δ (a), then the amount of cosmic dust in the column with height D (parsecs), with a base of 1 cm², and with a mass density δ (a) (grams per cm³) equals

$$3.08 \times 10^{18} \times D \times \delta \text{ (a) grams.} \tag{3}$$

Hence the amount of photographic extinction produced by this column is the product of (2) and (3):

$$\Delta m(ptg) = 1.39 \times 10^{23} \times D(pc) \times \delta \text{ (a) (gm/cm}^3) \tag{4}$$

Since

$$1 \text{ gram/cm}^3 = 1.46 \times 10^{22} \odot/pc^3, \tag{5}$$

formula (4) reads as follows:

$$\Delta m(ptg) = 9.5 \times D \times \Delta \text{ (a)} \tag{6}$$

In (6) we express D in parsecs and we call the particle density in $\odot$ per cubic parsec, Δ (a). (In these equations, *a* is the radius of the scattering grains.)

We can now estimate the particle mass of a globule with radius R(parsecs) and density Δ (a) ($\odot$ per parsec³). In terms of solar masses, we have:

$$M_{glob, \text{ particles}} = 4.19 \times R^3 \times \Delta \text{ (a)} \tag{7}$$

Because of the irregular shape of the globule, and since we are involved only in order of magnitude averages, we set D = 2R. Then from (6):

$$\Delta \text{ (a)} = \frac{\Delta m(ptg)}{19R} .$$

Substituting into (7) we have:

$$M_{glob, \text{ particles}} = 0.22 \times R^2 \times \Delta m(ptg). \tag{8}$$

In this formula, the derived value of the mass is measured in solar masses; R, the radius, in parsecs; and Δ m(ptg), the photographic absorption, in magnitudes.

For example, a globule with Δ m(ptg) = 10.0 and R = 0.4 pcs has a derived minimum particle mass equal to:

$$M_{glob, \text{ particles}} = 0.35 \odot.$$

TABLE 1

List of Representative Globules

Object	R. A. (1975)	Decl. (1975)	Approx. Diameter	Comments
IC 1848	3^h 01.0^m	$+60°$ $26'$	$1'$	Round, opaque globule associated with some nebulosity.
Barnard 34	5^h 41.8^m	$+32°$ $39'$	$20'$	Larger, isolated globule, with about 3 mag. absorption.
Barnard 227	6^h 05.9^m	$+19°$ $42'$	$10'$	Isolated globule with 5 mag. absorption.
(Rosette) NGC 2237—44	6^h 30.8^m	$+ 4°$ $53'$	$100'$	Emission nebula containing bunches of small globules. In Monoceros.
NGC 2264	6^h 39.9^m	$+ 9°$ $31'$	$1'$	Square, opaque globule within an elephant trunk structure. In Monoceros.
Barnard 255	17^h 19.1^m	$-23°$ $24'$	$6'$	Fairly transparent, round globule.
Barnard 68	17^h 21.1^m	$-23°$ $48'$	$3'$	Very opaque, smaller Barnard object found in region of Theta Ophiuchi.
(Trifid) NGC 6514	18^h 00.6^m	$-23°$ $02'$	$17'$	Small emission region containing several globules.

TABLE 1

List of Representative Globules (cont.)

Object	R. A. (1975)	Decl. (1975)	Approx. Diameter	Comments
(Messier 8) NGC 6523	18ʰ 01.8ᵐ	−24° 23′	90′	Emission nebula where globules were first pointed out.
Barnard 87	18ʰ 02.4ᵐ	−32° 30′	12′	More transparent object with streamers. South of the great star cloud in Sagittarius.
Barnard 92	18ʰ 14.2ᵐ	−18° 16′	12′	Opaque, elliptical object with projecting threaded filaments. Region in Sagittarius north of the great cloud.
Barnard 133	19ʰ 04.8ᵐ	− 6° 57′	7′	Opaque, elliptical globule found in Scutum.
Barnard 335	19ʰ 35.7ᵐ	+ 7° 31′	4′	Fairly opaque and round.
Barnard 361	21ʰ 11.9ᵐ	+47° 18′	20′	Round, isolated globule with about 3 mag. absorption.
Nebula near BD + 56° 2604	21ʰ 35.9ᵐ	+57° 23′		Not a globule. Squiggly nebulosity with an E-W length of 30′. Seems to have a shock front on the southern boundary.
Barnard 367	21ʰ 43.5ᵐ	+57° 04′	3′	One of several small condensations in a nebulous region.

Fig. 1. The 90-inch reflector of Steward Observatory at its Kitt Peak station, University of Arizona.

We note that the derived mass is a *minimum* mass, since it represents only an estimate for the particles of optimum size and scattering properties to produce extinction. *All* gaseous contribution, including HI and molecular hydrogen, are ignored. It is customary, following Bok (1956) and Spitzer (1968), to multiply the mass obtained from (8) by a factor 100, since the solid particles probably contain at most one percent of all the mass in the globule, the rest being in gaseous form. Applying this correction factor, we find that the most likely mass for the above globule is equal to 35 ⊙.

The regions with selected globules, accessible during the fall and winter of 1969–70, were photographed at the Cassegrain focus of the Steward Observatory 90-inch reflector at the Kitt Peak Station. The Cassegrain focus operates at f/9, with a resulting scale of 10″/mm. The unvignetted field at the Cassegrain focus has a diameter of 8 inches, 33′. For the globules of greatest interest we made three exposures of 60 minutes duration without image tube, the first on an Eastman 103a-O emulsion with GG13 Schott glass filter, the second on Eastman Special 098-02 emulsion (red sensitive) with RG2 filter, and the third on Eastman emulsion 103a-D with GG14 filter. When Eastman Special 098-02 emulsion was not available, we used Eastman 103a-E emulsion instead for our red exposures with RG2 filter. Bok (1969) has published information regarding relative speeds of Eastman Special 098-02 and 103a-E emulsions. Sample reproductions of photographs are shown in Figures 2, 3, and 4.

It seemed highly desirable to record for several of our globules stars fainter than are recorded in one-hour exposures by regular photography with our 90-inch reflector. For this purpose, we used the Carnegie image tube adapted for direct photography. For detailed information, we refer the reader to a technical report prepared by Cromwell (1969); because of our special interests, we shall describe the technique here briefly.

The image tube used in our work is a standard Carnegie image tube, an RCA C33011 2-stage cascade tube with magnetic focusing provided by a permanent magnet. Over-all operating voltage is about 21 kilovolts. The tube has an S20 photocathode that is sensitive from 3,000 A to 8,500 A. The useful field is 38 mm in diameter, which corresponds to 6.4′ at the f/9 Cassegrain focus of the 90-inch reflector.

The relay lens, used to transfer the phosphor output of the image intensifier to a photographic emulsion, is an 86 mm f/1.2 Elgeet Navitar operated at 1:1 magnification. The aperture is set at f/2 to reduce spherical aberration.

We use IIa-O emulsion for recording the Carnegie tube output. The exposure time used with the image tube to obtain a "sky-limited" exposure

Fig. 2. The globule Barnard 227. *Above:* a negative in the blue from the Palomar Observatory Sky Survey. *Below:* a negative in the blue from a 90-inch plate (B. J. Bok). The fields are approximately 35′ by 35′. North is up, east is left.

Fig. 3. The globule Barnard 361 as seen on a Palomar blue negative (above) and a 90-inch blue (below). The field is approximately 35′ by 35′. North is up, east is left.

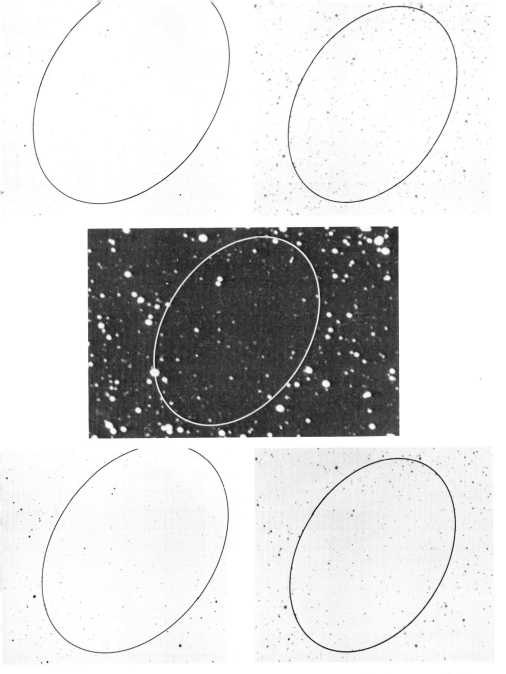

Fig. 4. The globule Barnard 34 (circled in each photograph). *Upper left,* 90-inch red plate; *upper right,* Palomar red; *middle,* Barnard atlas print; *lower left,* 90-inch blue; *lower right,* Palomar blue. The field dimension is about 35′ by 35′; north is up, east is left. The only positive print is from the Barnard Atlas (*middle*).

(that is, where the plate density is such that the faintest possible stars have been recorded) is about 1/10 that for unaided photography. This takes into account the relative speed, or "blackening rate," of the image tube and the unaided emulsion and also the difference in transmission of the respective filters. The limiting magnitude of an image tube record is about one magnitude brighter than that of an unaided photograph. The primary causes for this loss in limiting magnitude are an over-all mottled sensitivity pattern of the Carnegie tube (which seriously affects the signal-to-noise ratio of the threshold images) and a light-induced background produced by the image tube.

The filters used in the present study are a blue interference filter selected to suppress the radiation from the night sky (transmission is limited to a passband from 4,250 A to 5,450 A) and a stock thickness Corning 2-60 red filter (this produces a passband from 6,100 A to 8,500 A with an effective wavelength near 6,700 A). Sky-limited photographs are obtained in 30 minutes with the 90-inch f/9 Cassegrain reflector and the limiting magnitudes are respectively about 22 in the blue and 21 in the red. Sample image tube photographs are shown in Figures 5 and 6.

The globule Barnard 227 is an isolated globule, one of the finest on Barnard's list (1927); it is shown in Figure 2. Star counts in blue and red light were made for this globule and for a comparison field close to the globule but well outside its limits. These counts were made to the limits of the photographs from our 90-inch reflector plates. They yield a minimum value of 5 magnitudes for the total photographic absorption produced by the globule, but the indications are that the globule has a much greater total photographic absorption and that it may possibly be quite opaque. A rough distance to this globule can be determined on the assumption that all the stars seen in the direction of the globule are foreground stars. To achieve this, the distance to the globule would have to be of the order of 600 parsecs, and we have assumed this distance in all of our calculations. An argument in favor of assigning to this globule a very high total absorption is that we do not see any great masses of faint stars appearing in our globule photographs in red light. This is in marked contrast to the situation found by Bok (1956) in the dark nebula south of ρ Ophiuchi, for which large numbers of faint red stars are shown on the longest-exposure red sensitive plates. While the minimum photographic absorption assigned to the globule Barnard 227 is Δ m(ptg) = 5 magnitudes, a more likely value is Δ m(ptg) = 10. Assuming a radius R = 0.38 pc and Δ m(ptg) = 10, we find from formula (8) a minimum particle mass for the globule equal to 0.3 $\odot$. Applying the correction factor of 100, as explained above, we find for the most probable value of the mass 30 $\odot$.

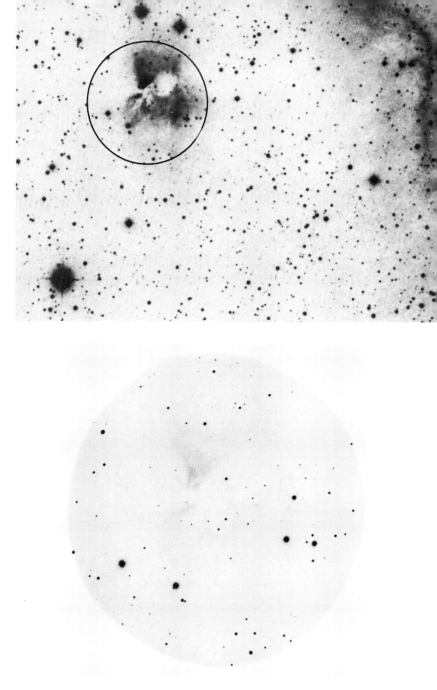

Fig. 5. Globule associated with IC 1848. The area circled on the Palomar red print *(top)* is the same field as shown by the 90-inch image tube print in the red *(bottom)*. The circled field has a diameter of approximately 6′. North is up, east is left. Negatives are shown.

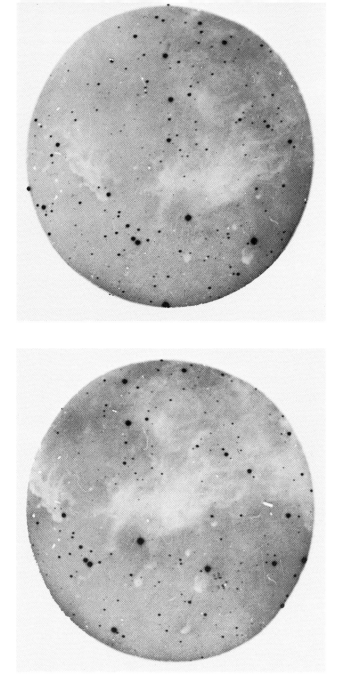

Fig. 6. Globules associated with NGC 2244. The photographs were taken with the 90-inch reflector using the image tube. The red negative print is on the top, blue is on the bottom. Each field has a diameter of about 6′; north is up, east is left.

It is of interest to speculate on the physical conditions inside a globule such as Barnard 227. The cloud with a total mass of 30 ⊙, and with a radius of the order of 0.4 parsecs, should have an average particle velocity of the order of half a kilometer per second. This value can be obtained by simple application of the Virial Theorem.

Since Barnard 227 is located close to the galactic plane, it will have interstellar gas from the galactic medium constantly passing through it. Some, if not all, of this gas will be captured by the globule in one way or another. The presumably very low temperature inside the globule, esti- mated to be of the order of $10°$ K, will encourage the formation and capture of molecules on the cold particles, which possess efficient mecha- nisms for dissipating the heat produced in such captures. If we assume an average turbulent velocity in the interstellar gas of 7 km/sec and an average density of the interstellar gas equal to 0.025 ⊙/pc^3, then the calculated total mass of interstellar gas passing through the globule in 10^8 years will be of the order of 9 ⊙. This figure represents the maximum rate of accretion experienced by this globule as a result of the passage of interstellar gas through it.

Table 2 and Figures 2, 3, and 4 give data for some of the larger globules studied in the present investigation. First on the list is Barnard 227, and it is followed by two rather comparable objects, Barnard 34 and 361. The latter two differ from Barnard 227 in that there are indications that they are semi-transparent. Barnard 34 and 361 contain more faint stars on the photographs in red light than would be expected if they were totally opaque. Hence we have assumed a total photographic absorption $\Delta m(ptg) = 2.5$ magnitudes for both objects. This value has been obtained by transforming the logarithmic deficiencies in star numbers into probable values of total photographic absorption expressed in magnitudes. We note that the minimum particle masses of these objects begin to come close to 1 ⊙ and that their most probable masses are respectively 70 and 50 ⊙. Orion 1 near $\alpha = 5^h 37.0^m$; $\delta = -1° 48'$, is a curious feature. It is shown especially well on the red Palomar print and has a bright emission rim directly to the south and east of it. It is shown as an empty blank spot on our 90-inch photographs of longest exposure in both blue and red light. This globule may resemble the Orion globules studied by Penston (1969). His globules have assigned masses of the order of 1 ⊙ and internal temperatures of the order of $10°$ K. Penston's globules appear to be slightly smaller in diameter than our Orion globule.

We have made rather extensive photographic studies of one of the globules associated with the emission nebula IC 1848; Figure 5. It is seen beautifully projected against the emission nebulosity shown by the red Palomar print. It is also seen quite readily in outline on the blue Palomar

TABLE 2

Large Globules

Object	Assumed Distance (pc)	Radius (pc)	Most Probable Mass (solar)	$\sqrt{\overline{V^2}}$ (km/sec)	Maximum Accretion in 10^8 Yr. (in solar mass)
Barnard 227	600	0.4	30	0.45	9
Barnard 34	600	1.1	70	0.41	66
Barnard 361	600	0.9	50	0.39	46
Orion	400	0.1	2.2	0.24	0.6
IC 1848	1700	0.3	20	0.42	5
NGC 2264	900	0.14	4	0.28	1.1

Notes: $\triangle$ m$_{ptg}$ assumed equal to 10 for all except Barnard 34 and 361.

$\triangle$ m$_{ptg}$ assumed equal to 2.5 for Barnard 34 and 361.

The Orion globule is near $\alpha = 5^h 37.0^m$, $\delta = -1° 48'$

TABLE 3
Small Globules

Object	Assumed Distance (pc)	Radius (pc)	Most Probable Mass (solar)	$\sqrt{\overline{v^2}}$ (km/sec)	Maximum Accretion in 10^8 Yr. (in solar mass)
NGC 2244	1660	0.02	0.1	0.12	0.02
		0.06	0.8	0.2	0.2
IC 2944	2200	0.005	0.01	0.07	0.001
		0.03	0.2	0.14	0.05
MESSIER 8	1260	0.02	0.1	0.12	0.02
		0.08	1.4	0.22	0.4

Notes: $\triangle m_{ptg}$ assumed equal to 10.

The two sets of numbers indicate data for the smallest and the largest globules of these nebulae.

print of the same region. Figure 5 shows both the red image tube photograph and the red Palomar print of this globule. These show it as a clearly delineated dark feature. The three stars seen in the direction of the globule are probably foreground stars.

We have taken several plates, with and without image tube equipment, of the globule shown near the head of the comet-like feature associated with NGC 2264. There is no sign of any stars shining through this globule, which is presumably at the distance of approximately 900 parsecs assigned to NGC 2264. We note that there are several "windblown" globules seen projected against parts of NGC 2264.

Some of the most interesting globules found are seen projected against bright emission nebulae. These are very small dark objects, and, whereas some of them have rough edges, others are almost perfectly round. Table 3 shows the available information for NGC 2244, IC 2944 and Messier 8. We have made a careful survey of the region of NGC 2244 for which we obtained image tube photographs in red and blue light; on the same plates we photographed as well a nearby comparison field relatively free from obscurations. The small globules are clearly delineated on the image tube photographs. Their radii are mostly in the range of 5,000 to 10,000 astronomical units, and their most probable masses lie between 0.1 and 1 $\odot$. Figure 6 shows image tube photographs of a 6′ diameter field in NGC 2244.

The globules associated with IC 2944 have been studied especially by Thackeray (1950), who was their original discoverer. They appear to have radii in the range between 1,000 and 6,000 astronomical units. A reproduction of a recent photograph is shown in Figure 7. The "most probable masses" assigned to these objects in Table 3 are obviously lower limits, for we have no way of telling what may be the density of interstellar grains and of associated gas in these objects. Masses of the order of 1 $\odot$ are of course not at all out of the question. Accretion will probably play a rather minor role for these very small globules.

The globules associated with Messier 8 were the subject of the original investigation by Bok and Reilly (1947), and these resemble in many respects the globules associated with NGC 2244. The original study of small globules by Bok and Reilly (1947) was made from a print of Messier 8 based on a photograph with the Lick Observatory Crossley reflector. W. Baade and R. Minkowski pointed out to Bok that most of the globules that appeared roundish on the Lick photograph seemed more irregular ("windblown," Baade) when inspected on Mount Wilson and Palomar photographs. This is confirmed by our recent 90-inch photographs. In many ways the objects noted by Bok and Reilly are more like the globules studied by Penston (1969) than they resemble the globules for NGC 2244 and IC 2944.

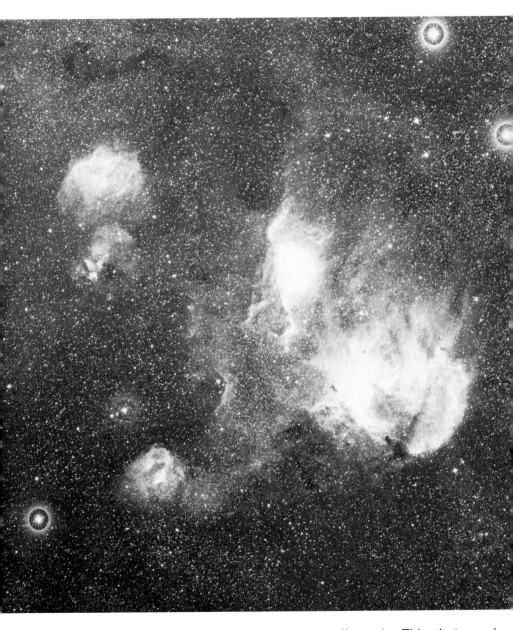

Fig. 7. IC 2944 showing globules as small specks. This photograph was taken at Cerro Tololo by B. J. Bok. North is up, east is right.

TABLE 4
Unit Cloud

ρ Ophiuchi (Dark Cloud)

Distance $= 250$ pc	Min. particle mass $= 21 \odot$
Radius $= 4$ pc	Most probable mass $= 2100 \odot$
$\triangle$ m $_{ptg} = 3^m - 8^m$	$\sqrt{\overline{v^2}} = 1.2$ km/sec
Maximum accreted mass in 10^8 yrs ∞ 900 $\odot$	

Table 4 summarizes as best we can the available data for the unit dark cloud near ρ Ophiuchi. The basic information has been obtained from the paper by Bok (1956). One of the most interesting facts associated with this dark nebula is that star counts make it possible to establish radial density gradients for this particular object. With its radius of 4 parsecs and a most probable mass of about 2,000 $\odot$, it seems like an almost ideal dark cloud about to collapse into a cluster of stars. This happens to be the dark nebula for which Heiles (1969, 1970) has determined the temperature from the intensity distribution in the OH bands; he finds that temperatures of the order of $5°$ to $10°$ K probably prevail in the interior parts. The plentiful supply of cosmic grains should provide an excellent mechanism for radiating away any excess heat produced through interaction with the surrounding interstellar medium; accretion will almost surely play here a very important and basic role. The study of the future evolution for this sort of unit dark cloud offers fine prospects for theoretical research.

In many ways the Southern Coalsack is not unlike the dark nebula near ρ Ophiuchi. Its dimensions and probable total mass are comparable to the values for the ρ Ophiuchi dark nebula. There is no such clear indication for a radial density gradient in the Southern Coalsack as there is for the other dark nebula and, offhand, the Southern Coalsack may well evolve by breaking ultimately into separate smaller units.

In recent years, astronomers studying early stages of stellar evolution have pressed the search for places in our galaxy where the beginnings of star birth may presently be observed. One suggestion that has been made seeks the origin of star birth in the centers of dense HII regions. According to Schraml and Mezger (1969), we find compact strong radio emitters of high electron density embedded in dense clouds of cosmic dust. Such concentrations are observed to occur most likely in giant HII regions.

Another approach suggests that the process of star birth is vigorously at work in the shock waves produced as a result of the density waves of the Lin-Shu density wave theory of spiral structure. Roberts (1969) has calculated that there should exist a high-density ridge inside each spiral arm, and he has expressed the opinion that star birth originates along this ridge.

Another suggestion has been that star birth is accelerated by shock waves originating from supernova outbursts. Observation suggests that star birth does not take place uniformly along the shock front but that the process is most active when the shock wave passes through gas concentrations with densities 10 to 100 times average.

Over the years, much evidence has accumulated to show that T Tauri stars are of very recent origin. The papers by Herbig have especially stressed the importance of T Tauri stars (Herbig, 1958). These stars are often found associated with dark nebulae, including some to which we have referred in the present paper.

To the above listing of possible places of star birth, we should now add the regions where the globules and the unit dark nebulae are found. Table 1 lists a number of representative globules which deserve further study by radio and optical techniques. The objects listed in Table 1 represent concentrations of interstellar matter which may be on the verge of, or in the process of, collapse leading to single or multiple star formation. The largest ones may well collapse into clusters of stars.

There are several varieties of globules. The first class of globules are the small objects of Table 3. Many of these are sharply bounded small units (NGC 2244, Fig. 6; and IC 2944, Fig. 7) with diameters in the range from 1,000 to 10,000 astronomical units. Others, notably the Orion globules studied recently by Penston (1969) and those associated with Messier 8, are of another variety. They can truly be said to be "wind-blown" and they have ill-defined edges. Both varieties of globules occur at the peripheries of HII regions. Herbig (1958) considers some of these to be snipped-off elephant trunks, but this explanation seems rather far-fetched when applied to the sharply delineated small globules, which have the appearance of dust balls compressed by pressure waves. We know of no observed concentrations of cosmic grains or of gas that seem more on the verge of collapse than do the smallest globules seen projected against the emission nebulosities of NGC 2244 and IC 2944.

The Barnard Objects of Table 1 are a very different variety of globules. Most of them are isolated units of cosmic grains with remarkably sharp boundaries. They stand out from their surroundings as well-defined globs of dust. Samples are shown in Figures 2, 3, and 4. It is difficult to understand how such units can have formed in our turbulent galaxy, but their presence cannot be denied. These objects deserve much closer attention than they have received to date. Optical astronomers must study them to the limits permitted by our giant reflectors. They are objects that must be investigated especially in the infrared, not only to determine the wavelength dependence of the absorption produced by them but also for the purpose of attempting to obtain possible measures of the integrated infrared radiation. With the high resolution made available by new radio astronomical techniques, we must press the search for associated 21-centimeter radiation, and every effort should be made to detect in the radio range effects produced by the molecules that must be associated with these objects.

The low temperatures found for the globules of the second variety, and the absence of ionized gas in their vicinity, are indicative of conditions that seem to favor collapse. It is well known that magnetic fields have a tendency to inhibit collapse in ionized regions, and this may be the reason why the smallest distinct globules are found outside the regions of greatest ionization in such nebulae as NGC 2244 and IC 2944. Presumably no strong magnetic fields are associated with such globules as Barnard 227, 34, or 361. In the initial stages of collapse, the dust grains in these isolated globules should serve as effective radiators of any produced excess heat. Hence, the chances are that collapse will proceed at first without any marked heating of the interiors of the isolated globules, and the possibilities for ultimate collapse are hence enhanced.

The observational evidence for the presence of globules in our galaxy is very encouraging to those of us who have been looking for years for places of possible star origin. If we did not actually observe globules, we would be inclined to postulate their existence!

Discussion

G. B. Field: These globules have a physical state very different from other interstellar clouds, and therefore one wonders whether the grains in the globules are normal or typical of the interstellar medium. Is there any information about whether the reddening curve in the globules differs in any way from that in the interstellar medium in general?

Bok: Not at this time. However, the present study lists several larger globules for which the faint stars are beginning to come through. For these globules, it should be a relatively straightforward project to determine from star counts the absorption in blue light and in red light. Image tubes should assist very much in this work. I would hope that our list of representative globules might be of value in future planning of such studies.

J. Greenstein: I recall that a man named Bok wrote a small paper in which he said, "Don't pre-judge the issue that the ratio of gas to dust is 100 in dark nebulae." I would think that there is still good reason to doubt that it is the same. The known mass of atomic gas is not large, and the conjecture made is that the gas is in molecular form. All efforts to find molecular hydrogen in the high concentrations required have failed. A rough order-of-magnitude calculation of the accretion rate, as given in these tables, provides an input energy large compared to the internal energy. Unless there is some radiation, depending on the distribution of grain sizes, I would guess that it would heat the grains.

Bok: If the heat were considerable, Frank Low would have seen it in the globules in the infrared. Isn't that correct?

F. Low: I would prefer to answer this later.

Bok: I have been encouraged by Heiles' observations, which were done in a region (ρ Oph) suggested by Weaver and which gave OH quite markedly and apparently right at the center of the same large darks clouds I studied fifteen years ago. These OH temperatures are very low.

N. Dieter: There is some indirect evidence of a large amount of molecular hydrogen in these clouds, whether we can see it or not.

D. Hollenbach: I question whether the molecular hydrogen can accrete on grains, since it is quite likely that all grains exist at temperatures greater than $4°$ K and molecular hydrogen cannot accrete unless the grains are at a temperature less than $3°$ K. Also, you have "equivalent densities" of at least 1,000 hydrogen atoms per cubic centimeter. Is this just the contribution from grains?

Bok: No, there must be grains and gas together. For the grains alone one obtains densities of the order of 10 to 100. Of course, the grain densities are tentative, too, because all we know for the majority of the globules is that we don't see through them. However, some, like B34 and 361 are not opaque. I should point out that Dr. Lynds' catalogue has a number of very good candidates for semi-transparency.

M. Werner: How many globules are there?

Bok: I would say that there are at least 100 small globules and 100 reasonably sized ones. The small ones can only be seen against emission nebulae, and there might be many more. Dr. Fleischer wrote a paper many years ago in which he gave evidence for thousands of globules in the Sagittarius region alone. That is a matter well worth following up.

Werner: Do you think that these globules are gravitationally collapsing?

Bok: My guess is "yes." Radiation pressure exerted by the outside field probably assists in the collapse. The good thing about a globule is that you see it already as a very small dark cloud. Some are no bigger than 10,000 astronomical units, and these are practically the size of a large solar system. I don't think that these small units have a choice other than collapse.

Low: Is the accretion of mass produced by the particles slowing down and being captured by sticking, or is it a gravitational effect?
Bok: Not gravitational, I would say. How it happens I don't know. The accretion we have calculated is clearly a maximum, because we have assumed that the globule holds all the gas that streams into it. If some of the gas streams through the globule, there would be less accretion.
Low: But do the molecules have to stick?
Bok: Yes, to provide accretion.
D. Harris: Do the statistics for globule distribution make it reasonable that there are enough of these things to form stars at the rate we observe?
Bok: The statistics of the distribution of globules over the sky is as yet unknown.

BIBLIOGRAPHY

Barnard, E. E. 1927, *Atlas of Selected Regions of the Milky Way,* ed. E. Frost and M. Calvert, Publ. Carnegie Inst. of Wash., no. 247.
Bok, B. J., and Reilly, E. F. 1947, *Ap. J.* 105: 255.
Bok, B. J. 1948, *Centennial Symposia,* Harvard Obs. Monograph no. 7, p. 53.
Bok, B. J. 1956, *A. J.* 61: 309.
Bok, B. J. 1969, Am. Astron. Soc. Photo Bulletin 1, p. 8.
Cromwell, R. H. 1969, Technical Report 38, Optical Sciences Center, University of Arizona.
Heiles, Carl 1968, *Ap. J.* 151: 919.
Heiles, Carl 1969, *Astr. Soc. of the Pac.* Leaflet no. 482.
Heiles, Carl 1970, *Ap. J.* 160: 51.
Herbig, G. H. 1958, *Stellar Populations,* ed. D. J. K. O'Connell, p. 127.
Hulst, H. C. van de 1949, *Rech. Astr. Obs. Utrecht,* vol. 11, part 2.
Khavtassi, J. 1955, *Bull. Abastumani Obs.* no. 18.
Lynds, B. T. 1962, *Ap. J. Supp. Ser.* 7: 1.
Penston, M. V. 1969; *M.N.R.A.S.* 144: 524.
Roberts, W. W. 1969, *Ap. J.* 158: 123.
Roshkovsky, D. A. 1955, *Contr. Alma-Ata* 1 (no. 1-2): 136.
Schoenberg, E. 1964, Veröffentl. Sternw. München, vol. 5, no. 21.
Schraml, J. and Mezger, P. G. 1969, *Ap. J.* 156: 269.
Sim, M. E. 1968, *Publications,* vol. 6, no. 8, The Royal Observatory, Edinburgh.
Spitzer, L. Jr. 1968, *Stars and Stellar Systems,* vol. 7, p. 6.
Stoddard, L. G. 1945, *Ap. J.* 102: 267.
Thackeray, A. D. 1950, *M.N.R.A.S.* 110: 524.
Thackeray, A. D. 1964, *I.A.U. Sym.* 20, Kerr and Rodgers, Ed. p. 19.

5. Polarimetry

AINA ELVIUS

Stockholm Observatory

The interstellar grains, which so efficiently dim the light from distant stars, do so in a selective manner, favoring certain wavelengths of light and usually also certain directions of light vibration. Starlight transmitted through a cloud of well-aligned, asymmetric dust grains is found to be linearly polarized.

This type of interstellar polarization was first reported by J. S. Hall (1949) and W. A. Hiltner (1949). During the twenty years following this important discovery a great number of investigations have been devoted to the polarization of starlight. Studies of the degree of polarization as a function of wavelength will help us to discriminate between competing theories of grain properties. Determinations of the position angles of the strongest light vibrations serve to map interstellar magnetic fields, if the polarization is due to the alignment of asymmetric grains in magnetic fields.

Light scattered by the particles in reflection nebulae is also observed to be polarized. This type of polarization was first observed about fifty years ago, when W. F. Meyer (1920) made rough measurements of the polarization of light in the Hubble nebula NGC 2261. The high polarization of this object has later been studied in more detail (R. C. Hall 1964). Polarimetric observations of other reflection nebulae will be discussed below.

The observations just mentioned pertain to objects within our own galaxy. Polarization effects in the Andromeda galaxy M 31 were first reported by Y. Öhman (1942) using a photographic two-channel polarimeter. More detailed polarimetric investigations of several galaxies have later been made by a number of observers using photoelectric technique.

Polarimetric measures of reflection nebulae in several colors show that the degree of polarization usually increases with the wavelength of light (Elvius & Hall 1966). In the nebulosity associated with Merope in the Pleiades cluster the degree of polarization also increases with the distance from the illuminating star. The same is true for NGC 2068 but not for NGC 7023, which is more irregular.

Several investigators have reported "radial" polarization in the nebulae studied by them. Exceptions to this rule have been noted for filamentary structures in the Merope nebula (Elvius & Hall 1967) and several nebulae observed by M. T. Martel (1958), where the direction seems to be related to the structure of the nebula.

Some computations of nebular models to explain the observed wavelength of polarization have been made by several authors. The most complete computations so far were recently made by Martha S. Hanner (1969), who studied several models, assuming various types of grains. Comparisons with observations were made only for the Merope nebula because of the complexity and small scale of other investigated nebulae. Hanner found a reasonably good fit with a model assuming dielectric grains with a size distribution of grain radii $n(a) = n_0 \exp[-5(a/O.6)^3]$, with the radius a measured in microns.

Some other models also seem possible: for example, dielectric cylinders of finite length and random orientation. The slightly higher polarization obtained in the computations of this model may be lowered by secondary scattering or dilution of light from other sources.

Curves computed by Hanner for silicate grains with impurities seem to offer other interesting possibilities that should perhaps be investigated further. Pure silicate grains, on the other hand, do not seem suitable because of their peculiar polarization curves.

Small graphite particles (like other very small grains) would give a much higher degree of polarization than is observed in the Merope nebula or in other ordinary reflection nebulae.

Several authors, mainly at the University of Arizona, have studied the wavelength dependence of polarization and have tried to interpret the results in terms of grain models. I would like to mention especially a paper by Serkowski, Gehrels, and Wiśniewski (1969), where an interesting relation between polarization and reddening was demonstrated. They could match both types of curves by assuming perfectly aligned infinite and smooth cylinders in accordance with earlier calculations by van de Hulst and others. The index of refraction as well as the average size of the particles were given individual values for each star. More realistic models with spinning grains could be used to explain the extinction curves for $m = 1.33 - 0.05$ i and with grain diameters of 0.2, 0.3, and 0.4 μ. The polarization curve for the star HD 24912, which is similar to the average polarization curve for many stars, could also be explained with this grain model. The more peculiar curves are difficult to interpret with such general models, however, because the theoretical curves tend to have a flattened maximum when the particles are distributed over a large range of sizes and are allowed to spin and wobble.

Computations of the polarization of light caused by silicate grains have been published by Wickramasinghe (1969), who compares his theoretical curves with the wavelength dependence of polarization observed by Coyne and Gehrels (1967). His results indicate that further investigations of similar grains may be of interest.

Some years ago the theory of graphite grains and ice-coated graphite grains was favored by some investigators. Now, however, it seems difficult to explain how such grains may be aligned in space. E. M. Purcell (1969) has pointed out that the diamagnetism of graphite is unfavorable for the magnetic relaxation process to work and to align the particles, as assumed in previous theories. This process is much more favorable for paramagnetic grains.

As mentioned before, the wavelength dependence of polarization as well as the reddening curve may differ from one star to the other or between different regions of the sky. It seems quite possible that these variations, at least partly, are due to differences in the optical properties of the dust grains, causing the reddening and polarization. I would like to point out here, however, that the position of the cloud relative to the star and the observer may play an important role, at least in the case of dense dust clouds.

Consider cases of different geometry but with the same distance R between star, S, and observer, O, and with the star behind a nebula of the same optical depth. The angular width of the aperture is the same in all cases. If $OC = R_1$ and $CS = R_2$, the brightness of a surface element of the cloud C will be roughly proportional to

$$R_1^{-2} \cdot R_2^{-2}.$$

This expression has a minimum for $R_1 = R_2 = 0.5R$. Therefore each element of the cloud contributes more scattered light when R_2 decreases from 0.5R toward zero. The total area of the cloud seen within the aperture is proportional to R_1^2 and therefore has a maximum when $R_1 \to R$.

Thus the two effects of cloud brightness and effective cloud area contribute to make the importance of scattered light proportional to R_2^{-2} and therefore increasing rapidly as R_2 approaches zero. This only expresses the well-known fact that reflection nebulae are situated very close to the illuminating stars. It may not have been noticed so often, however, that small dense reflection nebulae, which may be too inconspicuous to be studied as such, are sometimes included in the aperture during observations of color and polarization of stars. If the extinction is considerable, the contribution of scattered light from the nebula may change the colors and also polarize the light, if the nebula is asymmetric.

As an example I would like to mention VY CMa, which is known as a very peculiar object and which has been studied in detail with different techniques, all of which cannot be mentioned here.

Very high polarization of light of different colors was observed by Serkowski (1969 a) and independently by Shawl (1969). Later Serkowski (1969 b) made more measurements of this object and also of the polarization in the surrounding small reflection nebula. The polarization observed for the entire object is strongly dependent on wavelength, increasing toward ultraviolet, where it is observed to be of the order of 20 percent. In the jetlike nebulosity west of VY CMa the polarization was observed to be 40 percent.

The inclusion of the reflection nebula in the aperture when the entire object is measured will contribute to the observed polarization. Although the intensity of the outer part of the nebula is low, it seems plausible that nebulosity closer to the star is brighter and also polarizes the light in a similar fashion.

There is probably also an inner shell of still higher density which may polarize the light in the same sense. It may be ring-shaped rather than spherical. Let us make some rough estimates of the light scattered from this shell (or the innermost part of a dense nebula) to see if it can explain the observed polarization without being in conflict with the observed energy distribution.

Starting from the spectral energy distribution published by Hyland and associates (1969, Fig. 1), we may estimate the infrared energy emitted by the shell to be perhaps ten times the energy observed in the shorter wavelengths. This indicates that the absorption is heavy.

Most probably the total extinction is due to both true absorption and scattering. I would like to suggest a model where the observed light is mainly scattered light and only to a small percentage directly transmitted starlight. We may estimate the absorbed radiation to be of the order of 90 percent and the scattered radiation of the order of 10 percent. Directly transmitted starlight is assumed to be less than 1 percent.

Without specifying what kind of particles are present in the shell, we can assume that they have an albedo less than 1.0. For a given distribution of particle sizes the ratio of true absorption to scattering will increase with increasing wavelength, although the total extinction decreases with wavelength. The resulting color distribution and reddening law are therefore complex, and this may at least partly explain the unusual reddening curve derived by Hyland and associates.

The effects are unusually pronounced for objects with a shell of dust so dense that multiple scattering is important. The influence on colors and polarization will be much smaller for a thinner shell of a kind that may surround some other stars showing intrinsic polarization of a few percent or less. The color of the scattered light will be considerably bluer than the color of the transmitted starlight, although it will be redder than the original starlight. The color will probably become bluer with increasing angular distance from the star. This may be the explanation for the increase in polarization toward shorter wavelengths for which the radiation emanates from scattering further away from the star.

Asymmetry of the "shell" may also explain the difference in position angle in this model. If, namely, the main contribution to polarized light in a given color is a function of position along a curved structure that does not go exactly through the illuminating star, the position angle will vary along this curve. It seems probable that in VY CMa the UV light comes mainly from the outer parts where the polarization position angle is the same as in the reflection nebula further out. The blue, yellow, and red light may be scattered toward us mainly from parts of the shell closer to and more to the southwest of the object.

Soon after the discovery of interstellar polarization the strongest electric vectors were found to be roughly parallel to the galactic plane. The catalogue of 2,592 stars by J. S. Hall (1958) containing his own observations as well as data obtained by Hiltner and van P. Smith, showed clearly how the polarization varied with galactic longitude. Later observations have completed the picture of magnetic fields probably related to spiral arms in the solar neighborhood.

Thus the study of interstellar polarization may help us in interpreting other observations pertaining to galactic spiral arm structures, a field to which Bart Bok has contributed in several ways.

Polarization of light was observed also in the dark lanes of the galaxies NGC 5055 and NGC 7331 (A. Elvius, 1951, 1956) by photographic techniques using the double-image polarimeter constructed by Öhman. More accurate polarimetric observations of the Andromeda galaxy were made photoelectrically by Hiltner (1958) who measured the polarization of light from globular clusters shining through clouds in M 31. He found that the electric vector of the polarized light was generally parallel to the long axis of the galaxy.

Observations by A. Elvius and J. S. Hall (1964, 1965) showed polarization with the electric vectors parallel to the dark lanes in NGC 5128 and NGC 7814. In other objects observed by them, as well as in several galaxies (for example, M 81) observed by Appenzeller (1967), polarization was found in areas containing dark lanes or filamentary dark structures. At Mt. Stromlo Observatory in Australia Visvanathan (1966) observed 30 stars for polarization of light in the Large Magellanic Cloud. The observed polarization indicated that the alignment of particles was uniform over distances of the order of kiloparsecs, and it seemed to be related to the structure of the cloud. A maximum value of $P/A_v = 0.07$ was found, and an average $P/A_v = 0.05$, similar to the ratio of polarization to extinction found in our galaxy. I would like to cite here some words written a few years earlier by Bart Bok (1964), concerning possible magnetic fields in the Large Magellanic Cloud:

> The magnetic fields involved should measurably polarize light, and the search for such polarization is a primary current assignment for the optical astronomer. Preliminary observation by N. Visvanathan at Mount Stromlo has already demonstrated polarization of from 2 to 5 per cent in the light of some stars of the Large Cloud, but the work is only beginning. It is important to seek and study galactic magnetic fields; along with gravity they may act strongly on gas clouds and exert a pronounced influence on the structure and development of a galaxy.

Much stronger polarization has later been observed in the galaxy M 82 (Elvius 1963, 1969, Sandage & Miller 1964, Sandage & Visvanathan 1969). Although it is by no means clear that the polarization observed in M 82 can be due to scattering by interstellar dust, it may be of interest to mention this object here.

Three main mechanisms have been proposed to explain the polarization, which reaches about 30 percent in the outer filaments: (1) scattering by dust particles (Elvius 1963), (2) synchrotron radiation (Lynds & Sandage 1963), and (3) scattering by electrons (Solinger 1969a).

The assumption of optical synchrotron radiation was originally based on an extrapolation of the radio spectrum, which then seemed to be very flat. More recent observations (Kellermann & Pauliny-Toth 1969) show, however, that the radio flux density decreases much more rapidly with frequency than was anticipated. The extrapolated flux will be orders of magnitude too weak to explain the optical polarization.

Solinger explains the polarization in terms of Thomson scattering by free electrons in the ionized interstellar gas, heated by a shock wave from an explosion in the nucleus of M 82. He assumed a bright nucleus (similar to the nucleus of a Seyfert galaxy) illuminating the electron clouds. Recent observations in the infrared have confirmed the existence of a nucleus, south of the place first predicted by Solinger (1969 a, b). His model is quite interesting, although the necessary masses and electron concentrations are rather high. More discussion may be needed regarding the relation between the observed H α emission and the very high electron temperature assumed by him.

In view of such uncertainties I find it worthwhile to discuss also the possibility of light scattering by dust particles.

The observation by Kleinmann and Low (1969) of a prominent nucleus in the wavelengths 5 to 25 microns confirms the impression of considerable light extinction which is suggested by the many dark patches and lanes seen in photographs of M 82. Because of the strong extinction it is impossible to measure the brightness of the nucleus in optical wavelengths even with moderate accuracy. Thus it is not improbable that M 82 has a bright nucleus capable of illuminating clouds far from the main body of the galaxy. Rough calculations show that the observed light intensity and polarization may be explained in this way. It may be more difficult to explain the presence of dust so far from the center of the galaxy.

Discussion

H. Weaver: If you look at an object like the Merope nebula, is it possible to detect any polarization which rises from systematic grain orientations? The filamentary structure of the nebula delineates the outline of the particle alignment; might not there be some degredation of the polarization perhaps by other particles aligned through all the bulk of the line of sight?

Elvius: I think it is quite difficult to check. Of course you don't know exactly the original direction of polarization of light from the reflection nebula. The direction might be related to the direction to the illuminating star or to the alignment of particles in the filaments. It should perhaps be mentioned here that some of the stars behind the filamentary structure have been studied and they show polarization nearly opposite to that shown by the nebula.

Weaver: These would have to be very faint, rather late-type stars.

B. Zellner: Is there any theoretical basis for believing that even non-spherical grains will give polarizations that are not radial with respect to the radiating source?

Elvius: Yes, if you have elongated particles aligned in the filaments, they may influence the direction of the polarization.

Zellner: Has this been shown?

Elvius: This is what we (J. S. Hall and myself) tried to show for the Merope nebula. In Uppsala, I had expressed this hypothesis based on observations by Mrs. Martel, who had noted such effects in several nebulae which she had studied photographically.

Zellner: I realize that it is an observed fact, but has it been shown theoretically that aligned grains can do this?

Elvius: Yes, I think it has been shown theoretically. Martha S. Hanner gives numerical computations on this effect in her thesis (1969). No complete models for scattering by particles aligned in filaments seem to have been worked out so far, though.

REFERENCES

Appenzeller, I., 1967, *Publ. A.S.P.* 79: 600.

Bok, B. J., 1964, *Scientific American,* 210 (no. 1): 32.

Coyne, G. V., and Gehrels, T., 1967, *A.J.* 72: 887.

Coyne, H. G. V., and Wickramasinghe, N. C., 1969, *A.J.* 74: 1179.

Dahn, C., 1967, Ph. D. Thesis, Case Institute of Technology.

Elvius, A., 1951, *Stockholm Obs. Ann.* vol. 17, no. 4.

—————. 1956, *Stockholm Obs. Ann.* vol. 19, no. 1.

—————. 1959, *Arkiv f. Astron.* 2: 309.

—————. 1963, *Lowell Obs. Bull.* 5: 281.

—————. 1969, *Lowell Obs. Bull.* 7: 117.

Elvius, A., and Hall, J. S., 1964, *Lowell Obs. Bull.* 6: 123.

—————. 1965, *A.J.* 70: 138.

—————. 1966, *Lowell Obs. Bull.* 6: 257.

—————. 1967, *Lowell Obs. Bull.* 7: 17

Greenberg, J. M., 1968, *Nebulae and Interstellar Matter,* ed. B. Middle-hurst and L. H. Aller (Chicago: University of Chicago Press), Ch. 6.

Greenberg, J. M., and Roark, T. P., 1967, *Ap. J.* 147: 917.

Greenberg, J. M., and Shah, G. A., 1969, *Physica* 41: 92.

Hall, J. S., 1949, *Science* 109: 166.

—————. 1958, *Publ. U.S. Naval Obs.* 17: 275.

Hall, R. C., 1964, *Ap. J.* 139: 759.

—————. 1965, *Publ. A.S.P.* 77: 158.

Hanner, Martha S., 1969, "Light Scattering in Reflection Nebulae," Ph.D. Thesis, Rensselaer Polytechnic Institute, Troy, New York.

Hiltner, W. A., 1958, *Ap. J.* 128: 9.

—————. 1949, *Science* 109: 165.

Hyland, A. R., Becklin, E. E., Neugebauer, G., and Wallerstein, G., 1969, *Ap. J.* 158: 619.

Kellermann, K. I., and Pauliny-Toth, I. I. K., 1969, *Ap. J. Letters* 155: 71.

Kleinmann, D. E., and Low, F. J., 1969, *Bull. A.A.S.,* 1: 248.

Kruszewski, A., Gehrels, T., and Serkowski, K., 1968, *A.J.* 73: 677.

Lynds, C. R., and Sandage, A., 1963, *Ap. J.* 137: 1005.

Martel, M. T., 1958, *Suppl. Ann. d'Ap.* no. 7.

Meyer, W. F., 1920, *Lick Obs. Bull.* 10: 68.

O'Dell, C. R., 1965, *Ap. J.* 142: 604.

Öhman, Y., 1942, *Stockholm Obs. Ann.* vol. 14, no. 4.

Purcell, E. M., 1969, *Physica* 41: 100.

Sandage, A., and Miller, W. C., 1964, *Science* 144: 382.

Sandage, A., and Visvanathan, N., 1969, *Ap. J.* 157: 1065.

Serkowski, K., 1969a, *Ap. J.* 156: L139.
————. 1969b, *Ap. J.* 158: L107.
Serkowski, K., Gehrels, T., and Wiśniewski, W., 1969, *A.J.* 74: 85.
Shawl, S. J., 1969, *Ap. J.* 157: L57.
Solinger, A. B., 1969a, *Ap. J.* 155: 403.
————. 1969b, *Ap. J.* 158: L21 (& L25).
van de Hulst, H. C., 1957, *Light Scattering by Small Particles* (New York: John Wiley & Sons).
Visvanathan, N., 1966, *Mon. Not. R.A. Soc.* 132: 423.
Wickramasinghe, N. C., 1969, *Nature* 224: 656.

6. 21-cm Studies of the Association of Gas and Dust in the Galaxy

The relative distribution of gas and dust in the galaxy has been a matter of discussion for nearly two decades. There are two interrelated questions which we have to consider here. One concerns the ratio of gas to dust in the general interstellar medium, and the second concerns the ratio in highly obscured regions. General theoretical arguments had been put forward by Spitzer (1941), Savedoff (1953), and others that the dust grains are always dragged along by the gas particles during their motions. This had led to the expectation that concentrations of gas will also be concentrations of dust. However as stressed by Bok (1953, 1955) no convincing theoretical arguments have been put forward to suggest that the ratio of gas to dust has to be the same everywhere in the galaxy. Furthermore, it is generally assumed that in regions of high gas density, formation of new grains and molecules will occur, thereby modifying the ratio of gas to dust in such regions. We shall review here the observational data, from 21-cm studies, regarding the correlation of gas and dust in our galaxy and discuss the suggested interpretation of the observations.

The investigations of Lilley (1955) indicated for the first time a general correlation between the distribution of gas and dust. He showed that the peak brightness temperature of the 21-cm line profile was extremely well correlated with total photographic absorption over a range of 30 degrees in latitude in the direction of the galactic anti-center. The total photographic absorptions were the means according to Hubble's galaxy counts for l^I: 140° and 150°. The absorptions themselves were derived using the formula

$$\triangle m = 3.84 - \frac{1}{0.55} \log N, \tag{1}$$

where N is the number of galaxies. A similar correlation was also found for a strip at b^I: $-15°$ covering the region l^I: 110° to 200°. This latter strip intersected the dust extensions in Orion, Taurus, and Perseus. Lilley had also found that there is a similar correlation if one uses the total number of hydrogen atoms in the line of sight instead of only the peak brightness temperature.

The optical depth τ_{dust} is related to the photographic absorption $\triangle m$ by the expression (see Lilley (1955))

$$\tau_{dust} = \frac{\triangle m}{1.086} \, . \tag{2}$$

Also the peak optical depth of the 21-cm line is

$$\tau_{gas} = -\ln [1 - \frac{\triangle T_{max}}{T_K}], \tag{3}$$

where T_K is the kinetic temperature of the gas. From his observations at b^I: $-15°$, Lilley derived a relation between τ_{gas} and τ_{dust} of the form

$$\tau_{gas} = 0.14 \, \tau_{dust} + 0.22. \tag{4}$$

He further derived a relationship between the space density ratio of gas to dust and the ratio of the total number of gas atoms to the grains. The formula is

$$\frac{\rho_H}{\rho_D} = 1.48 \times 10^{-11} \frac{N_H}{N_G}, \tag{5}$$

where it has been assumed that the radius of the grain is 3×10^{-5} cm, the extinction efficiency is 2 and the internal grain density is 1 gm/cm^3. For regions of low τ_{gas} the value of N_H can be derived directly from observations of 21-cm profiles and with the knowledge of $\triangle m$ we can also compute N_G. Lilley derived an average value of 100 for the ratio ρ_H/ρ_D. However, as stressed by Bok (1955), the observed variation in the ratio was a factor of seven, and an average value under such conditions may not be very meaningful. Furthermore observations by van de Hulst, Muller, and Oort (1954), for two very dark regions in Taurus, by Heeschen (1955) of regions in Ophiuchus, and by Bok, Lawrence, and Menon (1955) of a number of very dark regions failed to show any significant correlation between increased optical absorption and enhanced 21-cm emission. On the contrary, Menon (1956) reported a significant decrease in 21-cm intensity in a region of high optical absorption in the direction of the cluster NGC 2264. The lack of correlation between gas and dust in such cases was interpreted as being due to the conversion of hydrogen gas into hydrogen molecules.

The observational situation was re-examined by Garzoli and Varsavsky (1966) who investigated the distribution of absorption from star counts and distribution of hydrogen from 21-cm profiles in a region in Taurus where there is a concentration of T-Tauri stars. They found a marked negative correlation between N_H and absorption A, corroborating the earlier result of Menon (1955) for a similar region. On the basis of the observed relation between N_H and A, they made an estimate of the amount of atomic hydrogen that must have condensed into molecular form on the assumption that the condensation of gas and grain should go together. For A $\approx$ 2 mag they estimated $N_{H2}/N_H \approx 5$. From this they concluded that regions of high obscuration should contain molecular hydrogen several times that of atomic hydrogen.

The unreasonableness of such a general conclusion was pointed out by Heiles (1967), who plotted N_H against τ_{dust} from the more extensive data of Van Woerden, Takakubo, and Braes (1962) and used Hubble's galaxy counts. It is not clear to me that any positive statement can be made on the basis of Heiles' plot. It seems difficult to believe that we can derive a correlation of the type found by Lilley on the basis of the more extensive data of Heiles. It is probably too unrealistic to expect that a single relationship between N_H and τ_G will apply to all regions at intermediate latitudes.

The possibility that the relationship between N_H and τ_G could be different for different regions was investigated by Varsavsky (1968). He chose the Taurus region already investigated by himself and Garzoli, and another small cloud in Ophiuchus studied by Mészáros (1968) that had been optically studied by Bok (1956). He considered the evolution of a cloud containing only atomic hydrogen and grains in which the ratio of N_H/N_G was the same everywhere. If we assume that subsequently molecular hydrogen is formed on the surface of the grains, the rate of the process would be proportional to the amount of grain surface per unit volume. Hence in regions of higher grain density N_H will decrease faster than in regions with lower grain density, and the ratio N_H/N_G will be smaller for higher values of N_G. The slope of the relationship between N_H/N_G and N_G is then a measure of the amount of hydrogen that has become molecular.

The plot of N_H/N_G against N_G for the regions in Taurus and Ophiuchus has very little scatter, and two straight lines can be fitted to the data. The extrapolation of the lines to N_G: 0 corresponds to the value of N_H/N_G when all hydrogen is atomic. For the two clouds Varsavsky finds

$$N_H/N_G \text{ (Taurus)} \approx 2 \times 10^{13}, N_H/N_G \text{ (Ophiuchus)} \approx 0.3 \times 10^{13}.$$

If the basic assumption regarding the formation of H_2 molecules is correct, then the slope of the relationship between N_H/N_G and N_G will be dependent on the time elapsed since the cloud was last ionized and the rate of formation of hydrogen molecules. The change of slope at $N_G \approx 8 \times 10^8$ cm^{-2} is interpreted by Varsavsky as being due to a slow-down in the rate of formation of molecules.

    The results of Heiles for the general interstellar field can also be plotted in the same manner. This has been done by Varsavsky, and the greater scatter for the general field is interpreted by Varsavsky as being due to the greater ages of the clouds involved as compared to the Taurus and Ophiuchus clouds. On the other hand the scatter also could be due to observational errors in the data and additionally to uncertainties in the basic assumptions made in the derivations of the numerical values of N_H and N_G.

    Of these uncertainties the most important refer to the assumption of uniform temperature in deriving N_H and assumption of same size for the grains in deriving N_G. Since the data plotted by Varsavsky refer to many different longitudes and latitudes, it is difficult to estimate quantitatively how much of the scatter is due to the above uncertainties.

    In order to check into this question more closely, further new observations were made using the 140' telescope (beam width 21') at Green Bank of the first section in Lilley's Figure 3 for longitudes l^{II}: 143° to 172° and b^{II}: −14°8'. 21-cm profiles with a frequency resolution of 7 KHz were obtained every one degree in longitude. Galaxy counts for this region are available in the Lick Observatory data of Shane and Wirtanen

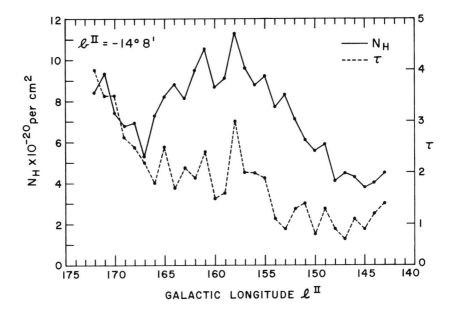

Fig. 1. N_H, the total number of hydrogen atoms per cm² as a function of galactic longitude.

(1967). The data have been converted into a convenient galactic coordinate distribution by Kiang (1968), and I have used these latter reduced counts and equations (1) and (2) in estimating the absorption optical depth. In those regions where no galaxies have been found I have assumed an absorption of 4 magnitudes. In computing N_{II} I have assumed that the optical depth in the 21-cm line is small. The plot of τ_G and N_{II} as a function of longitude is shown in Figure 1. It is apparent from the figure that there is a high degree of correlation between τ_G and N_{II} not only over the whole longitude range but even on a small scale of the order of two or three degrees. In Figure 2 I have plotted the ratio N_{II}/N_G as a function of N_G in the same manner as Varsavsky, and with the same assumptions.

If we look at the plot as a whole, there is considerable scatter, and we can at most say that a least-square line will give a value of between 0.2 and 0.3 x 10^{13} for N_{II}/N_G for N_G: 0. However the distribution of points in the graph suggests that we may divide the points into two groups, those with $N_G < 5$ x 10^8 and $N_G > 5$ x 10^8. The division also corresponds to longitudes $< 154°$ and $> 154°$. It is apparent that the least-square lines through the two groups will have quite different slopes.

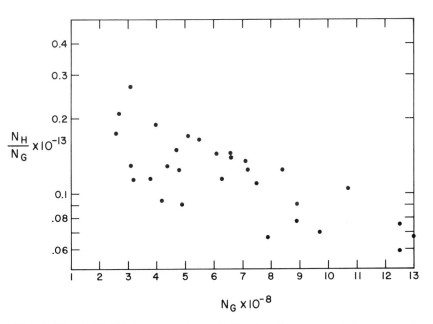

Fig. 2. The $I_n(N_{II}/N_G)$ versus N_G relation for the same strip covered in Figure 1.

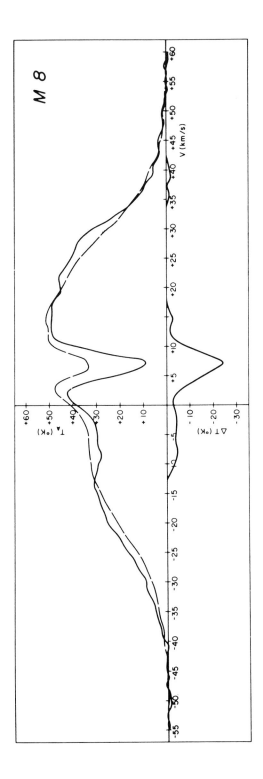

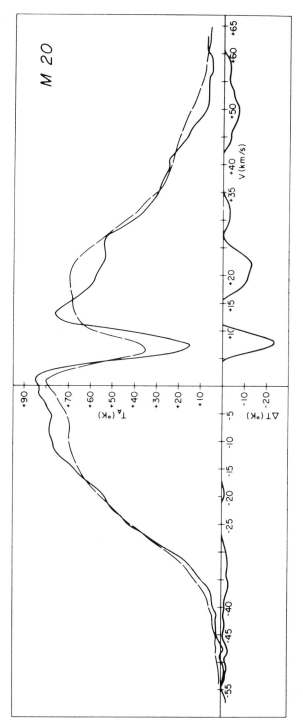

Fig. 3. The dashed curves are the expected 21-cm profiles determined by interpolating between profiles observed one beam width (20') on both sides of the sources. The continuous curves are the observed profiles in the direction of the source. The lower curves are the absorption profiles.

For the two groups we obtain values of approximately 0.3 x 10^{13} and 2.5 x 10^{13} respectively for N_{II}/N_G when N_G:0. These two values are almost exactly the same as that obtained by Varsavsky for the Ophiuchus and Taurus clouds respectively, even though the data used here have somewhat greater scatter.

On the other hand we cannot exclude the possibility of representing the data by a series of horizontal lines with different intercepts on the vertical axis. This is particularly so because of the overall correlation of Figure 1. As a matter of fact, except for 7 points, corresponding to high values of N_G the rest of the data on N_{II} vs. N_G plot can be represented reasonably well by a straight line.

From our discussion it would appear that the situation is not as clear cut as suggested by Varsavsky. There are a number of observational questions which can contribute to the state of confusion. Varsavsky's absorption data are based on star counts and should be considered only a lower limit when applied to the total line of sight for which the N_{II} value has been obtained. Where the absorption is high, as high as 8 magnitudes, the error in assuming that the absorption refers to the entire line of sight is probably not high. However for low absorption the error introduced in the absolute value of the absorption can be significant. The general effect of this error is to make the line drawn by Varsavsky for Ophiuchus more horizontal. The effect of lower kinetic temperature in regions of high obscuration is also to make the line more horizontal. Furthermore in the range of obscuration 2 to 5 x 10^{-8} N_G where Varsavsky obtains an intercept of 2 x 10^{13} our data show that we can at most obtain an intercept about 0.3 x 10^{13} similar to that of the Ophiuchus data of Mészáros.

Both Varsavsky and I have implicitly assumed that the ratio of gas to dust is not variable along a given line of sight. In view of the data on lateral variation shown in Figure 1 the assumption of constancy along the line of sight is certainly not justified. This would be particularly so when the absorption is determined from galaxy counts and could account for some of the scatter in Figure 2.

Another physical process that can produce an apparent decrease in the 21-cm emission in the direction of absorbing clouds is a lower kinetic temperature within these clouds. A priori it is, of course, not possible to distinguish between the effects of lower density and lower kinetic temperature. However in a few cases we have both 21-cm emission and absorption measurements of the same clouds. Figure 3 shows the expected emission profile and the observed absorption profile in the direction of two continuum sources M8, and M20. The prominent depression seen in the emission profiles is from a region which extends over 20 degrees in longitude and about 4 degrees or so in latitude near the galactic center. It is a cloud which was first studied in emission by Heeschen (1955) who suggested that the depression is due to absorption of 21-cm radiation from a hot cloud by a cold cloud in front of it. That his suggestion is basically correct is seen from the fact that the region of decreased emission has an optical depth of over 1 in absorption in the direction of the two sources.

From a comparison of the emission and absorption profiles we can estimate the kinetic temperature of the cold cloud to be about 30°K. We have no detailed information about the optical absorption over the whole region. It is interesting that the region of the cold cloud coincides approximately with the infrared source found by Hoffman and Frederick (1969). It is tempting to suggest that the infrared source is the dust formed in the cold cloud discussed above. On the other hand Menon (1970) has identified excess 21-cm emission from a dark cloud in the vicinity of the Orion Nebula. This excess is, however, not as much as one would have expected from the assumption of constant gas to dust ratio.

From the discussion so far we can make the following general statements. There is a general correlation in the distribution of gas and dust in the galaxy. In regions of low optical absorption the ratio of gas to dust shows only small random variations. However in regions of high optical absorption the ratio of gas to dust would appear to be smaller than expected. This apparent decrease in gas density may be due to lower kinetic temperature or lower abundance of the gas or due to both. In the present state of our knowledge there does not appear to be any clear observational evidence for the existence of any significant amount of molecular hydrogen in the general interstellar medium.

The observations reported in this paper were made while the author was a member of the staff of the National Radio Astronomy Observatory.*

Discussion

F. Drake: You have been interpreting the depletion of hydrogen in dense clouds as molecular formation at low temperature. At low temperature, isn't it as good a conclusion that there is a high optical depth (greater than one)? This may be due to low temperature, as you are also saying, but it could also be due to clumping; for example, maybe clouds have internally fragmented and then collapsed. This would give a high optical depth also.

Menon: Yes, but the clouds in such cases will have to be very small ones because we are talking about beam widths of the order of 20 minutes of

*The NRAO is operated by Associated Universities, Inc., under contract with the National Science Foundation.

arc or more. So it is not the larger typical Heiles clouds that you are referring to but much smaller ones.

Drake: It could be that these very dense clouds, because of the state they are in, have internally fragmented into large numbers of small clouds, yet are still spread out over what we call a single cloud.

Menon: Yes.

P. G. Mezger: Where is the emission of the 21-cm line in this area of Orion?

Menon: It is displaced by about 15^s of time from the center of the Orion Nebula, to the east.

REFERENCES

Bok, B. J. 1953, in *Gas Dynamics of Cosmic Clouds* (Interscience Publishers, New York), p. 221.

————. 1956, *Ap. J.* 61: 309.

Bok, B. J., Lawrence, R. S., and Menon, T. K. 1955, *Publ. A.S.P.* 67: 108.

Garzoli, S. L., and Varsavsky, C. M. 1966, *Ap. J.* 145: 79.

Heeschen, D. S. 1955, *Ap. J.* 121: 569.

Heiles, C. 1967, *Ap. J.* 148: 299.

Hoffman, W. F., and Frederick, C. L. 1969, *Ap. J.* 155: L9.

Kiang, T. 1968, *Dunsink Obs. Publ.* 1: 109.

Lilley, A. E. 1955, *Ap. J.* 121: 559.

Menon, T. K. 1956, *Astr. J.* 61: 9.

————. 1970, *Astronomy and Astrophysics,* 5: 240.

Mészáros, P. 1968, *Ap. and Space Sci.* 2: 510.

Savedoff, M. P. 1953, in *Gas Dynamics of Cosmic Clouds* (Interscience Publishers, New York), p. 218.

Shane, C. D., and Wirtanen, C. A. 1967, *Publ. of Lick Obs.* vol. 22, part I, p. 1.

Spitzer, L. 1941, *Ap. J.* 94: 232.

van de Hulst, H. C., Muller, C. A., and Oort, J. H. 1954, *B.A.N.* 12: 117.

Varsavsky, C. M. 1968, *Ap. J.* 153: 627.

Woerden, H. van, Takakubo, K., and Braes, L. L. E. 1962, *B.A.N.* 16: 321.

7. Interstellar Molecules

NANNIELOU H. DIETER

Radio Astronomy Laboratory
University of California, Berkeley

Fifteen years ago, in 1955, Bart Bok's Harvard students were observing interstellar neutral hydrogen with the 24-foot antenna at Agassiz Station; and, although that is not a very long time ago, not one of us would have predicted then the developments in radio spectroscopy that have filled the years to 1970. The pace of discovery has, in fact, been growing exponentially. Between the first observation of the hydrogen line in the interstellar gas in 1951 and the observation of $O^{16}H$, twelve years elapsed. Three years later, in 1966, the $O^{18}H$ molecule was found. The discovery of NH_3 in the fall of 1968 was followed in the winter of the same year by the discovery of H_2O. By spring of 1969 (a few months later) H_2CO was observed, and by summer the C^{13} formaldehyde molecule. No one can guess what the coming months will bring.

The list of new molecules observed tells only part of the story. Fully as important as our knowledge of the presence of these constituents in the interstellar gas is the resultant change in our view of the nature of the interstellar medium. In retrospect it is clear that these newly discovered molecules have upset the naive picture that had been engendered by the simplicity of the hydrogen atom. The fact that in the 21-cm line we were dealing with a single line that was collisionally excited and that had a very low transition probability led us into the belief that the interstellar gas was really rather simple. Although we knew, as Eddington wrote in 1927, that "Interstellar space is at the same time excessively cold and decidedly hot," collisional excitation of the line meant that we could ignore the problem because the maximum brightness temperatures measured in the line were determined by the local kinetic temperature. Also, most of the exploitation of the hydrogen line was related to galactic structure, a use that depends primarily on the combination of low optical depth but high abundance of the element rather than on local physical conditions.

*This work was supported by National Science Foundation Grant GP-14356.

In the past seven years since 1963, we have begun to recognize how little we know. When the discovery of absorption in the 1667 MHz line of the OH molecule (Weinreb and others 1963) was followed by observation of the weaker 1665 MHz line with the intensity expected on the basis of equilibrium conditions, all appeared to be in order. There was the disturbing problem of understanding the formation of the molecule, but our ignorance of the specific nature of interstellar grains allowed us to escape the difficulty by assuming that an oxygen and a hydrogen atom could combine on the surface of a grain (possibly a correct assumption). A further problem was the absence of evidence for the OH molecule in optical spectra of interstellar lines — one that remains despite concerted efforts to detect its ultraviolet lines.

These somewhat minor problems were overshadowed in 1965 when emission from the OH molecule was found (not by design but by chance) (Weaver and others 1965). The strength of the 1667 MHz line in emission led us to try to observe also the weaker 1665 MHz line, which, of course, turned out to be extremely and anomalously bright. This surprise was followed by a series of others — the complexity of the detailed structure of the lines and the extreme sharpness of some features, the unpredictable strength in different sources of the two additional satellite lines, the high degree of polarization of some features (Weinreb and others 1965; Palmer and Zuckerman 1967), and the unbelievable fact that they varied significantly in intensity in a period of weeks (Weaver and others 1968). High angular resolution observations showed some of these OH emission sources to be fantastically small — thousandths of a second of arc — and consequently with fantastically high brightness temperature, $10^{12}°$K (Moran and others 1968). All these things suggested that excitation of the OH emission lines occurs by maser action in the interstellar medium — an absolutely unexpected result. Attempts to identify the pumping mechanism driving this maser activity have been fraught with difficulty, and the most positive conclusion at this time seems to be that in order to explain the appearance of OH in different places, near thermal sources, near nonthermal sources, and near infrared stars, for example, not one mechanism but several are required.

The search for new constituents in the interstellar gas went on, despite our ignorance of how they are formed. CH was the most likely candidate, since it has been observed optically. Uncounted hours of observing time were spent in the unsuccessful search for radio lines of this molecule. Others were suggested by Townes (1957) in his paper "Microwave and Radio-frequency Resonance Lines of Interest to Radio Astronomy." He listed a dozen molecular rotation lines followed by the cautionary remark: "Probably only the diatomic molecules of the table exist in detectable abundance in space." Among the entries in the table were NH_3 and H_2O. The remark was certainly occasioned by astronomers' belief that the probability of formation of molecules with more than two atoms was vanishingly small.

In 1968 we learned that we knew less than we had thought about the formation of molecules, when emission lines of ammonia were found (by Townes and his colleagues at Berkeley) in directions near the galactic center (Cheung and others 1968). Although extensive searches have been made in other regions, ammonia has been found nowhere else. The excitation of the ammonia lines is probably collisional so that the excitation temperature reflects the kinetic temperature. In this case, as opposed to the H-line, five lines are available — and the ratio of the line intensity of any two of these yields the kinetic temperature — which should, of course, be the same for any combination of lines. The temperatures determined from the ratios of the (1, 1) line to the (2, 2) and to the (3, 3) lines are not the same, differing in the same direction in the sky by as much as a factor of three (Cheung and others 1969a). This observation leads the authors to conclude that the nonequilibrium intensities "reflect, in a way at present unknown, events in the past history of the cloud." We must, therefore be concerned not only with the present condition but also with the history of the gas — another facet of the problem that we had largely ignored.

Detection of the (6, 6) transition in NH_3 was a surprise even to the discoverers of the molecule in the interstellar gas because the energy of the upper level corresponds to a very high temperature, $400°K$. Its detection led them to look for a very unlikely line of H_2O, the (6, 6) transition with an upper-level energy equivalent to a temperature of $670°K$. They found it first in Sgr B2 (Cheung and others 1969b) and subsequently in seven other sources. In many ways the emission resembles the anomalous OH emission: the locations in which it appears, the presence of many narrow spectral features in each source, the extremely small angular size and high brightness temperature, and the variation in intensity over short time periods (Knowles and others 1969). As one might expect, however, the similarities are not complete. For example, the degree of polarization is much less than in OH, and, although the two molecules occur as nearly as can be measured in the same place (Meeks and others 1969), the velocity features in their spectra show no direct relation to each other. An interesting question to be answered is whether there is any discernible similarity in intensity variation in the two molecules within the same source. In addition, the problem of the pumping mechanism for the maser action in this H_2O transition is an even more difficult one than for OH. The high level transition probably cannot be excited simply by photon absorption but must be excited by collisions, and the source of the collision rate must be time dependent to explain the variations (Knowles and others 1969). All this suggests a dynamic, complex nature for the interstellar gas.

To further upset preconceived notions, formaldehyde was found in the interstellar gas in 1969 (Snyder and others 1969). The problem of molecular formation became still more puzzling since it was now established that polyatomic molecules containing two atoms other than hydrogen can form in the interstellar medium. Also, further investigation (Zuckerman and others 1970) showed that the formation apparently does not require extremely unusual interstellar conditions since CH_2O was detected in many places and with densities comparable to that of OH. Furthermore, all the polyatomic molecules observed, NH_3, H_2O, and CH_2O can be photodissociated by ultraviolet photons with energy less than 13.6 eV, so that they must be shielded by interstellar dust in order to survive (Feldman and others 1969).

The first observation of interstellar formaldehyde was the absorption of the (1, 1) rotational transition in the spectra of radio sources, many of the same sources in which OH had been detected in absorption (Goss 1968). What appears to be normal OH *emission* had also been found in cold, dark, dust clouds (Heiles 1968), and they were therefore likely candidates for finding CH_2O emission. No such emission was found. Formaldehyde appeared instead in absorption in these clouds, in directions in which no discrete radio-frequency sources exist (Palmer and others 1969). The authors were led to conclude that the CH_2O molecule is absorbing the isotropic 2.8°K primordial background radiation. The amount of absorption measured requires that the excitation temperature of the (1, 1) transition of CH_2O be less than 2.8°; in fact, that it be the improbably low value of 1.8°K. Townes and Cheung (1969) propose that such a temperature requires an excess population in the lower state of the transition and a non-thermal cooling mechanism, just as maser action in OH or H_2O requires a nonthermal excitation mechanism. They proposed molecular collisions with subsequent spontaneous transitions to the lowest level as the source of the excess population. Not only is this still another evidence of markedly nonequilibrium conditions in the interstellar medium, but it has another intriguing result. It confirms the deduction derived from the ammonia radiation (Cheung and others 1968) that a very large density of colliding particles must be present. The particles are very likely to be molecular hydrogen, and there must be one thousand of them per cubic centimeter. They, of course, have eluded positive detection and present the most challenging of observational problems.

I have described the succession of new results not only to emphasize that the more we find out the less we seem to understand, but also to suggest that the combination of information about the interstellar medium from many different avenues of approach can be fruitful in gaining a true understanding. I should now like to propose a model for one of the sources of molecular lines which draws upon a wide variety of observations and techniques. The model is probably wrong, is certainly inadequate, and requires from the listener more than anything else a "suspension of disbelief." My purpose in presenting it is to suggest the power of even the fragmentary information we now have.

The model describes the area of Sgr B2, a thermal radio source that lies about one degree from the galactic center. It is invisible optically because of the heavy obscuration, but is certainly an HII region. It is reported (Lequex 1967) to extend 2′ x 5′ to half intensity with an emis-

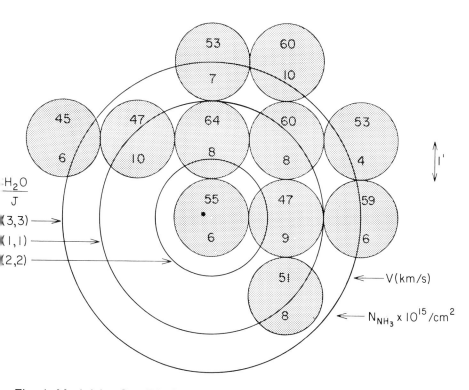

Fig. 1. Model for Sgr B2. Small circles indicate NH_3 observations. The larger circles represent the beamwidths used to observe the CH_2O transitions indicated.

sion measure of 8×10^5 cm^{-6} pc (Mezger and Henderson 1969), about one-third the brightness of the Orion Nebula. The maximum electron density is 300 cm^{-3}, and the radial velocity as measured in the H 109 $\propto$ radio recombination line is $+61.6$ km/sec (Mezger and Höglund 1967). This appears to be a rather ordinary galactic source, but the great richness of its molecular features make it quite an extraordinary one. I shall first describe briefly the observations of molecular lines associated with the source and then describe the model to fit them.

The OH absorption in Sgr B2 occurs at two widely separated velocities, -90 and $+60$ km/sec, with the very large velocity dispersion characteristic of the galactic center region, about 50 km/sec (Weaver 1970; Robinson and McGee 1970). The positive velocity feature (which coincides with the velocity of the HII region) is the one of interest here. It is produced by an unusually large number of OH molecules along the line of sight to the source, approximately 10^{16} molecules/cm^2 (assuming an excitation temperature of $3°K$). Very recently Gardner and others (1970) have observed the O^{18}H absorption in Sgr B2. The $+60$ km/sec feature, upon comparison with O^{16}H observations, shows a ratio of O^{18}H/O^{16}H that is greater than the terrestrial O^{18}/O^{16} ratio: $1/203$ compared to $1/489$. The interstellar ratio is derived on the assumption that the OH cloud uniformly covers the continuum background source. If this assumption is wrong, and the distribution is patchy and includes areas of high optical depth in the O^{16}H line, the ratio will be smaller and therefore closer to the expected value. This view of a patchy distribution of clouds has been proposed by several authors and forms the basis for the present model.

The emission of the ammonia molecule in this direction has been most completely delineated by Cheung and others (1969a) with 2-minute angular resolution. They observed the three lowest level inversion transitions at 2-minute intervals over a region about $8' \times 14'$ centered on the continuum source. As mentioned above, they found the excitation temperatures derived from ratios of pairs of these lines to lie between $10°$ and $100°K$ and to be inconsistent with equilibrium conditions. In each different direction they also determined the number of NH$_3$ molecules along the line of sight and the central radial velocity of the emission. The amount of ammonia varies from 0.4 to 1.0×10^{16} molecules per cm^2 in different directions, a surface density comparable to that of OH. The velocity varies in the directions measured from $+45$ to $+64$ km/sec, with no obvious systematic dependence on position. It is this map of the Sgr region that I shall use as the geometrical basis for the model.

Sgr B2 was one of the first sources in which interstellar formaldehyde was detected. The spectrum of the (1, 1) transition measured by Zuckerman and associates (1970), with 6-minute resolution, shows seven velocity components, the strongest of which has a radial velocity of $+61.6$ km/sec, in agreement both with the recombination line and OH velocities. The same authors were also able to detect in Sgr B2 the $+62$ km/sec feature in the similar transition of $C^{13}H_2O$ (Zuckerman and associates 1969). Their comparison of observations of the two isotopes led them to some interesting conclusions. The shapes of the profiles of the two varieties of formaldehyde agree within the limits set by the noise level. If the formaldehyde is distributed uniformly over the entire source, the $C^{12}H_2O$ profile should be about 10 percent wider than the corresponding $C^{13}H_2O$ profile because of the large optical depth in the $C^{12}H_2O$ line. One interpretation of the similarity in the two profiles is that the formaldehyde is not distributed uniformly but is clumped in condensations of large optical depth. The observed profile would then correspond to the distribution of the velocities of the condensations. Zuckerman and associates also point out that the ratio of the abundance of C^{13} formaldehyde to C^{12} formaldehyde observed in the direction of Sgr B2 is surprisingly large. The ratio is based on the assumption of a uniform distribution of all the gas. The ratio, $C^{13}H_2O/C^{12}H_2O$, has the value in Sgr B2 of $1/8.6$, while the terrestrial abundance ratio, C^{13}/C^{12}, is $1/89$. If, however, the assumption of uniform distribution is abandoned, they state that the discrepancy can be resolved by postulating the existence of small condensations each with a maximum optical depth of 14 in the $C^{12}H_2O$ line and altogether covering only 57 percent of the source. This conclusion is, of course, reminiscent of the conclusion reached in the discussion of the ratio of $O^{18}H/O^{16}H$, in which a patchy distribution of OH gas would bring the deduced interstellar O^{18}/O^{16} ratio closer to the terrestrial ratio. There is, in the formaldehyde case, the additional evidence of the similarity in line widths for the two different isotopes that can best be explained by several clouds overlapping in velocity.

We may now turn to the detailed observations of $C^{12}H_2O$ in different rotational transitions as a source of information on this cloud of molecules near Sgr B2. Each has been made with a different beamwidth and so covers a different area of sky. I shall make the assumption that the excitation temperature of the lowest of these levels (1, 1) is the low value of $2°K$ found in dust clouds at other places in the galaxy (Palmer and others 1969). The assumption is, in essence, that in front of and near Sgr B2 there is dense obscuring material. This is surely not unreasonable since such a large population of molecules probably needs the shielding afforded by such material to survive.

As already mentioned, Zuckerman and others (1970) observed the (1, 1) CH_2O transition in Sgr B2. At the center of the line profile they found the background continuum intensity to be reduced by 0.52. The normal deduction is then that

$$\frac{T_{\text{line}}}{T_{\text{cont}}} = 0.52 = 1 - e^{-\tau} ; \tau = 0.85$$

where T is antenna temperature and τ, the optical depth in the line. This calculation is based on the assumption that all the area of the continuum source that lies within their 6-minute beam is covered uniformly by gas of the same optical depth. We may now compare this result with that from the higher level (2, 2) CH$_2$O transition.

Evans and others (1970) observed this transition in Sgr B2 with a 3-minute beamwidth. The radial velocity and line width they found to be the same as that in the (1, 1) line. Although one would expect the absorption to be weaker in the higher level line, they found

$$\frac{T_{\text{line}}}{T_{\text{cont}}} = 0.67 = 1 - e^{-\tau} ; \tau = 1.1$$

The assumption of uniform coverage of the source by clouds again leads to improbable results. This comparison of (1, 1) and (2, 2) lines made with 6' and 3' beams, respectively suggests that the 6-minute beam includes parts of the continuum source that are not covered by clouds. The unabsorbed continuum radiation then reduces the apparent optical depth in the line. The 3-minute beam more closely conforms to the size of the absorbing cloud and one therefore derives a more realistic optical depth in this line. As Evans and others showed, one can predict the optical depth in the (2, 2) line on the basis of the (1, 1) value and the assumption that the isotropic background temperature of 2°7 is the pertinent one to determine the 2 mm radiation temperature. This is the radiation that presumably raises the CH$_2$O from the (1, 1) to the (2, 2) level. The ratio of optical depths is typically between 0.1 and 0.3 for excitation temperatures of the lower level between $1°$ and $10°$.

These, then, are the observations of Sgr B2. We can now devise a specific model and compare predictions made on the basis of it to the observations. Let us assume that $\tau = 14$ in the (1, 1) line for each cloud, as deduced from the C^{13}/C^{12} ratio, and that the distribution of such clouds has the form shown in Figure 1. Suppose that the gas, containing all the molecules, is distributed within the circles filled with dots. (The continuum source Sgr B2 is considered to be just larger than the outer envelope of the collection of circles.) These circles represent the 2-minute-diameter beamwidth with which the ammonia was observed. Each of these is thought of as a separate cloud with the velocities indicated in the upper part of each circle. These are velocities measured in NH^3 spectra.

(The lower numbers indicate the numbers of ammonia molecules along the line of sight in each cloud [Cheung and associates 1969a].) The larger circle, marked (1, 1), indicates the 6-minute beam with which the $C^{12}H_2O$ and the $C^{13}H_2O$ lowest level transitions were measured. One can see that if the formaldehyde were contained within these clouds defined by the circles, the profiles for both molecules would be composed of components with differing central radial velocity, but, of course, each wide enough in velocity to overlap the next. The profiles of the two isotopes could under these circumstances have the same width, as is observed.

Also in the figure, 60 percent of the area of Sgr B2 that is included within the 6-minute beam is covered by clouds. Zuckerman and associates (1969) found that if the small condensations cover 57 percent of the source the interstellar ratio of C^{13}/C^{12} derived would be identical to the terrestrial one. The model is also entirely consistent with the amount of absorption observed in the (1, 1) $C^{12}H_2O$ line. There the ratio of line intensity to continuum intensity is 0.52, that is, the background radiation is reduced by 52 percent. If the optical depth is very large (14, for example), this suggests that 52 percent of the source is covered by the dense formaldehyde condensations. As stated, the model indicates 60 percent, and in this rigid and unrealistic model, that can be considered agreement.

We can now compare the results of observations of the (2, 2) formaldehyde line with the model. The observations were made with a beamwidth of three minutes of arc, indicated by the inner circle marked (2, 2). Under the various assumptions stated above, the optical depth in this line predicted from the value in the (1, 1) line is 4.5. The observed ratio of line to continuum intensity is 0.67. Therefore, 67 percent of the 3′ beam should be covered by formaldehyde clouds. Examination of the figure shows that 60 percent of the beam (which is completely covered by Sgr B2) is covered by clouds. In other words, the model is consistent with this observation also.

We may also predict the optical depth to be expected in the still higher level (3, 3) formaldehyde line. If $\tau = 14$ in the (1, 1) line for each cloud, it should approximately equal one in the (3, 3) line. If we observe this absorption with an 8-minute beamwidth (labeled (3, 3) in the figure), uniform coverage of the part of the source included within the beam would give a line to continuum ratio of 0.63. The incomplete coverage shown by the model clouds reduces the expected ratio to 0.5. We shall see soon, I hope, whether the model survives this test also. All the results support the view that Sgr B2 qualifies as an extraordinary object.

It is, however, apparently not unique. Nearby in the sky lies another region that may be examined with the same sort of model in mind. This is a region a few minutes south of the galactic center where the background continuum source is Sgr A, the bright nonthermal source thought to be associated with the center of the galaxy. There is apparently in this case some confusion concerning the exact position of the molecular cloud. It is of interest here partly because it illustrates the power of the technique of lunar occultation measurements of spectral features.

The survey of the galactic center region in the ammonia lines (Cheung and others 1968) showed that emission was present at a position about 3′ south of the Sgr A position. The cloud was shown to be less than 5′ in diameter and to have a radial velocity of +23 km/sec. Somewhat later Kerr and Sandqviṣt (1968) observed a lunar occultation of the galactic center region and found an absorbing cloud of OH about one and a half minutes of arc away from the Sgr A position. The feature has an average radial velocity of +37 km/sec and an angular size of 3′ x 5′. Toward the southern part of the cloud the velocity is less than the average (14 to 24), and closer to the NH_3 velocity.

Zuckerman and associates (1970) looked for CH_2O absorption in the galactic center region including Sgr B2 and the position near Sgr A at which NH_3 had been found. They detected with their 6′ beam $C^{12}H_2O$ (1, 1) absorption with $T_{line}/T_{cont.} = 0.10$. In approximately this position Zuckerman and associates (1969) also detected $C^{13}H_2O$. They found as in Sgr B2, an unexpectedly large ratio of intensity of the C^{13} to C^{12} varieties, and in this case found that if the $C^{12}H_2O$ cloud has an optical depth equal to 8 and covers 10 percent of the source the terrestrial C^{13}/C^{12} ratio will be duplicated. Evans and others (1970) also found (2, 2) level absorption in the same position. They found $T_{line}/T_{cont.} = 0.15$, again larger than for the presumably stronger (1, 1) line.

It is quite possible for one to reconcile the two observations if the formaldehyde occurs in a small cloud, again 2′ in diameter, that lies entirely within but not centered in the 6′ beam (and covers, therefore, one-tenth the area of the beam). In this picture it is also not centered precisely in the 3′ beam used for the (2, 2) observations. If the center of the cloud lies about one and a half minutes away from the center of this beam approximately 16 percent of the beam will be covered by the cloud and the ratio of line to continuum intensity in the (2, 2) transition will be accounted for.

In fact, there is independent evidence that the center of the cloud is displaced by about this amount. Kerr and Sandqvist (1970) in June 1969 observed a lunar occultation of the region in the (1, 1) formaldehyde line in the same way that they had earlier observed OH in this region. They find the positions of the OH and CH_2O clouds to be the same within 0°5 and to be not three minutes, as indicated in the NH_3 observations, but one and a half minutes south of Sgr A. They also find the CH_2O cloud to be apparently (although not positively) smaller than the OH one, that is, in the one direction they can measure it is about 1' in diameter rather than 3'. This dense cloud is certainly the one observed in both the (1, 1) and (2, 2) observations. Since in each of the observations described the central position of the beam was actually displaced one and a half minutes from the center of the cloud, the observations are compatible with a very large optical depth in this cloud. It is in many ways similar to the ones postulated for the Sgr B2 region.

We should, of course, examine the physical nature of the clouds proposed for both sources. Each cloud is 6 parsecs in diameter, if they are all considered to be 10 kpc away. It has in it OH, NH_3, and CH_2O, each molecule with approximately the same surface density, 10^{16} molecules/cm^2. (This is surprising considering the very different nature of the molecules, and may hold clues toward solving the mystery of their formation.) This means that each has 6 x 10^{-4} molecules/cm^3 of each species. Indirect evidence from study of the excitation on NH_3, OH in dust clouds, and the anti-inversion of CH_2O in the same clouds suggests that there is also a density of hydrogen molecules equal to 10^3/cm^3.

We should not conclude that we have truly described these objects without remembering that they include a region of very high excitation. The location of the OH and H_2O emission region near the galactic center is indicated by the small square in the figure (Raimond and Eliasson 1969). The size of the square does not reflect the size of the emitting region, since each of the two OH features with velocities of +74 and +68 km/sec are very small, 0.1'' in diameter. This has been demonstrated both by long baseline interferometry (Rogers and others 1967) and by the effect of interplanetary scintillation (Robinson and Goss 1968). As nearly as can be told, the H_2O at +69 km/sec lies in the same direction as the OH (Knowles and others 1969). The OH brightness temperature is 7 x 10^9°K, and the linear size of the object is 5 x 10^{-3} pc or one thousand astronomical units. A feature in the H_2O spectrum at a radial velocity of +36 km/sec (close to the velocity characteristic of the more normal material of the region) seems to have been present in January 1969 and to have disappeared by February. Such extremes of activity and appearance engender humility in the maker of simple models.

Discussion

T. K. Menon: The velocities of some of the components you mentioned suggest regions of violent activity. Molecular formation is supposed to take place in comparatively quiet regions. What is your interpretation of this apparent discrepancy?

Dieter: Our assumptions about the formation of molecules have certainly pervaded the literature. Dr. Townes in 1965 published a classic paper on what lines to look for in the interstellar gas. We've all looked at it and used it. There is a table in the paper, at the bottom of which is a comment to the effect that it is very unlikely that any molecules other than the diatomic molecules in this table would be present in sufficient abundance to be detected in the interstellar gas. Both ammonia and water are listed, and Dr. Townes was instrumental in finding both.

C. H. Townes: I have one comment on this. In addition to the complications which Dr. Dieter has so very well discussed and brought together, there are some others too. In particular, I am reminded that, in the case of formaldehyde, one gets trapping of the radiation which connects the 1-1 state and the 2-2 state indicated here. Hence if the cloud is rather dense and small, the trapping tends to warm up the effective temperature and increase the abundance of the excited states further, so that when one puts in higher localized concentrations, this changes the temperature automatically. Thus one might have a rather large cloud of formaldehyde with clumps that become a different temperature from the rest of the cloud and give some additional complications to the general pattern. Because of this effect, as well as others, the excited states of formaldehyde may show up with a center of gravity quite different from the center of gravity of the ground states. I think that Evans, Cheung, and Sloanaker measured the position of the excited states of formaldehyde as agreeing with the ammonia position, that is, the one which is 3 minutes south. If lunar occultation shows that the ground state is only 1½′ south, these results are not necessarily inconsistent because of the temperature inhomogeneities.

P. Solomon: We have actually mapped the excited state of formaldehyde, and we find that the distribution is similar to ammonia and extends a little bit further than you have it. It is true that the formaldehyde does drop off a little to the east (we say 60 percent), and that the velocities are different from the ammonia value and that the peak of maximum optical depth is found in a different location.

Dieter: Are these different enough that you can explain the C^{12}, C^{13} width?

Solomon: The observed profiles of the C^{12} and C^{13} do not have the same shape; there is an asymmetry in the C^{13} which is not present in the C^{12}.

Dieter: I see, the model doesn't last very long!

Solomon: Your model of using a filling factor (the usual astronomical fudge factor) which we all use is probably right, but I'm not sure that the clumps of the molecules aren't really much smaller.

P. G. Mezger: In making models of objects like Sgr B2, one should be aware of the fact that these HII regions, which are obviously quite close to the galactic center, are certainly not HII regions of the normal spiral arm variety. Firstly these HII regions have enormously high internal velocities, as we can see from the recombination line profiles, which show bumps and asymmetries which are not found in any spiral arm HII region. Another peculiarity of these HII regions close to the galactic center is their apparent deficiency in helium, again as determined from recombination line observations of the He 109 and He+173 lines.

Addendum:

In the first paragraph of this chapter, I stated (fortunately) that no one could guess what the coming months will bring. As of February 1971 they have brought the discovery of eight new molecules in the interstellar gas, *twice* the number known at the time of the symposium! The newly observed molecules are: CO,[1] CN,[2] H_2,[3] CH_3OH,[4] HC_3N,[5] $HC^{12}N$,[6] $HC^{13}N$,[6] H_2CO_2.[7] All but H_2 and HCN have been observed in Sgr B2, and many have been seen in other sources as well. In addition, further studies of NH_3[8] have been made in the region of the galactic center, and the (3,3) line of CH_2O[9] has been detected in Sgr B2 with a line-to-continuum ratio of 0.7.

(1) Wilson, R. W., Jefferts, K. B., and Penzias, A. A. 1970, *Ap. J. Letters* 161: L43.

(2) Jefferts, K. B., Penzias, A. A., and Wilson, R. W. 1970, *Ap. J. Letters* 161: L87.

(3) Carruthers, G. R. 1970, *Ap. J. Letters* 161: L81.

(4) Ball, J. A., Gottlieb, C. A., Lilley, A. E., Radford, H. E. 1970, *Ap. J. Letters* 163: L203.

(5) Turner, B. E. 1971, *Ap. J. Letters* 163: L35.

(6) Snyder, L. E., and Buhl, D. 1971, *Ap. J. Letters* 163: L47.

(7) Zuckerman, B., Ball, J. A., and Gottlieb, C. A. 1971, *Ap. J. Letters* 163: L41.

(8) Knowles, S. H., and Cheung, A. C. 1971, *Ap. J. Letters* 164: L19.

(9) Welch, W. J. 1971, *Bull. A. A. S.* in press (abstract).

REFERENCES

Cheung, A. C., Rank, D. M., Townes, C. H., Knowles, S. H., and Sullivan, W. T., III. 1969a, *Ap. J. Letters* 157: L13.

Cheung, A. C., Rank, D. M., Townes, C. H., Thornton, D. D., and Welch, W. J. 1968, *Phys. Rev. Letters* 21: 1701.

Cheung, A. C., Rank, D. M., Townes, C. H., Thornton, D. D., and Welch, W. J. 1969b, *Nature*, 221: 626.

Eddington, A. S. 1927, *Stars and Atoms* (New Haven: Yale University Press).

Evans, N. J., II, Cheung, A. C., and Sloanaker, R. M. 1970, *Ap. J.* 159: L9.

Feldman, P. A., Rees, M. J., and Werner, M. W. 1969, *Nature* 224: 752.

Gardner, F. J., McGee, R. X., and Sinclair, M. W. 1970, *Astrophys. Letters* 5: 67.

Goss, W. M. 1968, *Ap. J. Suppl.* 15: 131.

Heiles, S. 1968, *Ap. J.* 151: 919.

Kerr, F. J., and Sandquist, A. 1968, *Astrophys. Letters* 2: 195.

Kerr, F. J., and Sandqvist, A. 1970, *Astrophys. Letters* 5: 59.

Knowles, S. H., Mayer, C. H., Cheung, A. C., Rank, D. M., and Townes, C. H. 1969, *Science* 163: 1055.

Lequex, J. 1967, in *Radio Astronomy and the Galactic System,* ed. by H. van Woerden, IAU Symposium No. 31 (New York: Academic Press), p. 393.

Meeks, M. L., Carter, J. C., Barrett, A. H., Schwartz, P. R., Waters, J. W., and Brown, W. E., III. 1969, *Science* 165: 180.

Mezger, P. G., and Henderson, A. P. 1967, *Ap. J.* 147: 471.

Mezger, P. G., and Höglund, B. 1967, *Ap. J.* 147: 490.

Moran, J. M., Burke, B. F., Barrett, A. H., Rogers, A. E. E., Ball, J. A., Carter, J. C., and Cudaback, D. D. 1968, *Ap. J. Letters* 152: L97.

Palmer, P., and Zuckerman, B. 1967, *Ap. J.* 148: 727.

Palmer, P., Zuckerman, B., Buhl, D., and Snyder, L. E. 1969, *Ap. J. Letters* 156: L147.

Raimond, E., and Eliasson, B. 1969, *Ap. J.* 155: 817.

Robinson, B. J., and Goss, W. M. 1958, *Astrophys. Letters* 2: 5.

Robinson, B. J., and McGee, R. X. 1970, *Austral. J. of Phys.* 23: 405.

Rogers, A. E. E., Moran, J. M., Crowther, P. P., Burke, B. F., Meeks, M. L., Ball, J. A., and Hyde, G. M. 1967, *Ap. J.* 147: 369.

Snyder, L. E., Buhl, D., Zuckerman, B., and Palmer, P. 1969, *Phys. Rev. Letters* 22: 679.

Townes, C. H., 1957, in *Radio Astronomy,* ed. by H. C. van de Hulst, IAU Symposium No. 4 (Cambridge: Cambridge University Press), p. 92.

Townes, C. H., and Cheung, A. C. 1969, *Ap. J. Letters* 157: L103.

Weaver, H. (in preparation).

Weaver, H., Dieter, N. H., and Williams, D. R. W. 1968, *Ap. J. Suppl.* 16: 219.

Weaver, H. F., Williams, D. R. W., Dieter, N. H., and Lum, W. T. 1965, *Nature* 208: 29.

Weinreb, S., Barrett, A. H., Meeks, M. L., and Henry, J. C. 1963, *Nature* 200: 829.

Weinreb, S., Meeks, M. L., Carter, J. C., Barrett, A. H., and Rogers, A. E. E. 1965, *Nature* 208: 440.

Zuckerman, B., Buhl, D., Palmer, P., and Snyder, L. E. 1970, *Ap. J.* 160: 485.

Zuckerman, B., Palmer, P., Snyder, L. E., and Buhl, D. 1969, *Ap. J. Letters* 157: L167.

8. The Composition of Interstellar Dust

JOHN E. GAUSTAD

University of California, Berkeley

Let me first ask one question: Who cares what the interstellar dust is made of? The typical optical astronomer couldn't care less, for if you simply tell him the reddening law, particularly the ratio of total to selective extinction, he can unredden his clusters, correct the distance moduli, find the turnoff points, determine the age of the galaxy, and be happy! If this were the only astrophysical importance of the dust, I would stop now.

However, Mrs. Dieter has presented one good reason for caring about the composition of the dust: the mere existence of large numbers of interstellar molecules. It is very difficult to form molecules in space by direct two-body encounters, because the excess energy and momentum must be carried away by radiation of a photon, which is a relatively improbable process. The idea has therefore grown up that dust grains play a catalytic role in the formation of molecules. Atoms from the gas collide with a dust particle and stick to the surface for awhile, long enough to find another atom and react to form a molecule; the excess energy and momentum is then absorbed by the solid matrix of the particle. Surface chemistry is a complicated affair, difficult enough to study in the laboratory where one can use clean surfaces of known composition; and it seems to me almost impossible to develop a theory of molecule formation on interstellar grains without knowledge of the base material on which reactions are taking place. If globules accrete mass, the degree of accretion must certainly depend on the nature of the grain surface.

The second reason I am interested in the composition of the dust is the role it plays in the evolution of protostars. The dust plays an important role in determining the heat balance of a protostar in the early stages of its gravitational collapse. After a cloud becomes opaque to starlight, ions recombine and the normal cooling mechanisms of interstellar clouds become ineffective. Before the cloud becomes so dense that molecular lines are sufficiently pressure-broadened to be effective radiators, the con-

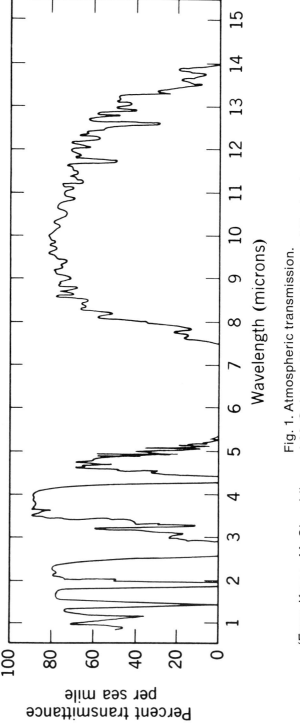

Fig. 1. Atmospheric transmission.

(From Kruse, McGlauchlin, and McQuistan, *Elements of Infrared Technology*, Wiley, p. 164)

tinuum radiation by the solid particles is the most effective mechanism for dissipation of the thermal energy generated by the collapse. As Bok has pointed out, radiation by the dust may also be a mechanism for keeping globules cool. The thermal history of the protostar (how much of its gravitational energy it loses during the collapse) will determine where it ends up on the "observable" H-R diagram. It may also determine the degree of fragmentation of an initially large protocluster, because as long as the temperature and the pressure remain low, subcondensations should be able to form. Now to calculate the radiative efficiency of the dust particles, we certainly need to know their composition, because at low temperatures most of the radiation will take place in the far infrared, where the emissivity is complicated by the band structure of the molecules within the grains.

It seems to me that in order to determine the composition of the dust, we must turn to the infrared part of the spectrum; it is here that the fundamental vibration-rotation bands of molecules lie. Such bands retain their identity even when the molecules are in the solid state. The rotational structure is smoothed out, and some wavelength shift and changes in intensity do occur; but the fundamental interaction is between neighboring nuclei within the molecule, which is relatively unperturbed by the presence of other nearby molecules. In contrast, the electronic band structure of a molecular gas may be completely changed in the solid state and become virtually unrecognizable.

What should we look for? The standard van de Hulst model of ice grains is perhaps the first thing to be tested. This model is based primarily on abundance considerations. Since carbon, nitrogen, oxygen, and hydrogen are the most abundant elements in stars (except helium which we would not expect to find in a solid state), one would not be surprised if solid grains in space consisted primarily of solid methane, ammonia, and water. Of these, water-ice should be the easiest to detect spectroscopically, because not only is it expected to be the most abundant molecule in the grains, but also the intensity of the fundamental O-H stretching vibration is increased by a factor of thirty in going from the gas to the solid phase, due to strong hydrogen bonding between neighboring molecules. This hydrogen bonding also shifts the wavelength of the band center from 2.7 to 3.1 microns, which is rather fortunate, for otherwise the absorption by the water vapor in the earth's atmosphere would make it completely impossible to observe interstellar ice from a ground-based observatory.

Even 3.1 microns (Fig. 1) is still in the wings of the telluric water band, and the atmosphere is only about 10 to 20 percent transmissive. The first attempt to detect the ice-band was therefore made from above the atmosphere, with Princeton's Project Stratoscope balloon telescope. Only one reddened star, Mu Cephei, was observed, however, and an upper limit of 25 percent was set on the ice content of the dust in this direction. It has since been shown that some of the reddening of this star may be due to circumstellar matter; thus the result is in any case not very conclusive for the interstellar dust.

More recently several other reddened stars have been observed from the ground at Lick Observatory. They are VI Cygni 12, CIT 11, HD183143, and 119 Tauri. In none of them has an ice band been found, and in the best cases an upper limit of about 10 percent can be set on the ice content of the dust. Figure 2 shows the spectrum of the heavy-reddened star VI Cygni 12. The solid lines show the expected transmission for pure ice grains: one curve is labeled with $A_v = 9.7$ which is the measured visual absorption for VI Cygni 12, the other curve represents the maxi-

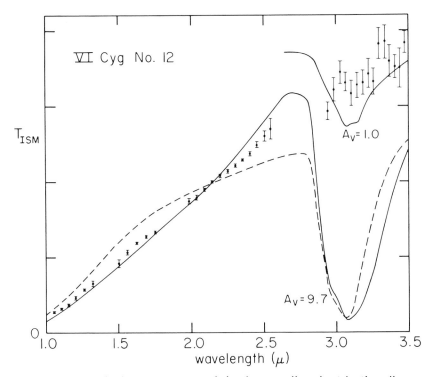

Fig. 2. Transmission spectrum of the interstellar dust in the direction of VI Cygni, no. 12. (From Knacke, Cudaback, and Gaustad, *Ap. J.* 158: 154, 1969)

mum absorption allowed by the observations. The dotted curve represents an ice-coated graphite model. These results are based on fairly good laboratory data; quantitative intensity measurements of pure ice extend down to 20°K. Mixtures of water-ice with methane and ammonia have not been studied quantitatively in the laboratory; but from other experiments, one does not expect the intensity of the water band to be changed or shifted appreciably unless the concentration of water molecules drops below a few precent. Specific observational tests for ammonia and methane in the grains are not yet possible, because the intensities of their fundamental bands are over an order of magnitude less than that of water-ice. However, more sensitive detectors and better observing techniques may soon give us some information on these molecules.

Let us turn now to another problem, the possibility that silicates may be an important constituent of the interstellar dust. Silicon. is, after all, the next most abundant element after nitrogen, and there are some places in the universe (such as the Tucson desert) where silicate dust is known to be very abundant. The first evidence for silicates in space was the discovery of an excess radiation near 10 microns in the spectra of several cool M stars, as illustrated in Figure 3. This emission is interpreted as originating from a cool circumstellar cloud of dust. As seen from comparison with the 300-degree black body curve in Figure 3, the

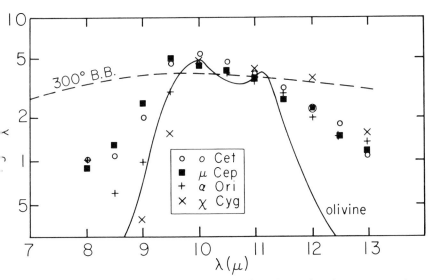

Fig. 3. Emission spectra of circumstellar dust clouds compared to that of olivine. (Based on observations of Woolf and Ney, *Ap. J.* 155: L181, 1969)

spectral distribution is much narrower than that of a black body at low temperature, so that the shape of the spectrum is likely determined by the spectral emissivity of the dust. The Si-O stretching vibration is at 8.2 microns in the gas phase. All solid silicates have strong bands due to this fundamental vibration somewhere in the 8 to 10 microns region, as illustrated by the emission spectrum of olivine $[(Mg, Fe)_2 Si O_4]$ shown in Figure 3.

These circumstellar clouds may or may not have anything to do with the interstellar dust; but I think they do, for two observational reasons. First, in the center of the Orion Nebula there is infrared emission with almost exactly the same spectral characteristics as the dust around the M stars (Fig. 4). Here is a region where, if anything, dust is being destroyed, not made; thus we may conclude that this observation is telling us something about the interstellar dust. Secondly, there is the one observation

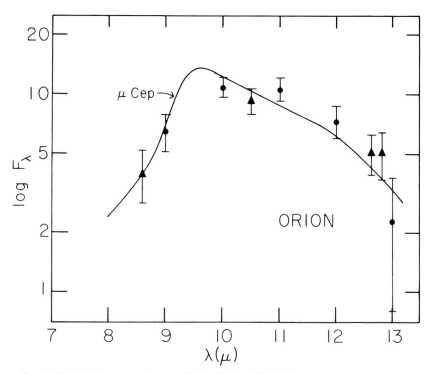

Fig. 4. Emission spectrum of the Orion Nebula compared to that of circumstellar dust clouds. (From Stein and Gillett, *Ap. J.* 155: L197, 1969)

of an absorption band at 9.7 microns in the spectrum of the reddened M supergiant, 119 Tauri, as illustrated in Figure 5. This band is most likely interstellar in origin, since it does not appear in unreddened stars of similar spectral type. Again, this can be reasonably identified with absorption by a silicate component of the interstellar dust, as illustrated by comparison of the absorption spectra of enstatite [(Mg, Fe) Si O$_3$] and olivine [(Mg, Fe)$_2$ Si O$_4$].

Can silicates be the entire story for the dust? At first thought it would seem not, for in order to produce an extinction of a magnitude per kiloparsec, about 1 percent of the mass in the interstellar medium must be in solid form, and silicon itself makes up only 0.06 percent of the mass. However, if one takes a complex silicate mineral, with two oxygen atoms for every silicon, throwing in all the magnesium, iron, sodium, aluminum, calcium, and other elements found in silicates, with another oxygen to

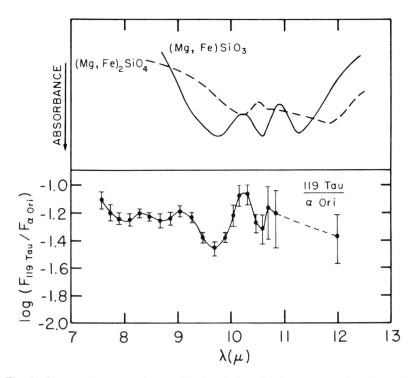

Fig. 5. Absorption spectrum of interstellar dust compared to that of silicates. (From Knacke, Gaustad, Gillett, and Stein, *Ap. J.* 155: L189, 1969)

go along with each, one can make up a grain containing about 0.5 percent of the total mass. Couple this with the higher index of refraction of the heavier elements, and you indeed will be able to build a grain model that will account for a major fraction of the extinction. The situation is even better if there is more hydrogen, perhaps molecular in form, in the galaxy than currently thought.

One should recognize that the possibility of graphite grains also still exists, although I have little to say about this possibility, since infrared spectroscopy is unlikely to provide any definite information about a non-molecular solid like graphite. Looking for electronic band structure of graphite in the ultraviolet may be a way of getting a positive identification, and indeed the rocket and OAO observations do seem to show a peak at about 2,200 Å which may be identified with a characteristic of graphite. However, farther down in the ultraviolet, graphite becomes much more transparent than the observations will allow, so that cannot be the entire story either.

I should like to conclude with a word of caution against jumping on the bandwagon of any particular model at the moment, for there may be many other possibilities for the chemical form of the solid particles in space which have yet to be considered or perhaps even discovered.

If we take an abundant element like carbon, for example, there are many other forms it might take than just graphite. It is conceivable that there are astrophysical conditions under which diamond particles might be formed, and one can find a size distribution of diamonds which will allow matching of the extinction curve over a wide range of wavelengths. Secondly, an entirely new allotropic form of carbon has been discovered recently, which the discoverers call "white carbon." It forms only at high temperatures and very low pressures, but again there may be astrophysical conditions where this would form preferentially to graphite. Little data are available on this substance, but it might prove an interesting possibility to consider.

Also, many new forms of water have been discovered recently. A polymeric form of water is under very active discussion in the literature now. It does not have any strong bands at 3 microns, but instead has its fundamental vibrations near 6 and 7 microns. If this were solidified in the interstellar grains, our current observations would not show it, for the 7 micron region is completely unobservable from the ground.

Still more recently, a "superdense" water-ice has been discovered. It forms only at low pressures and temperatures less than $100°K$, conditions which are just what you might find in interstellar space. However, in the laboratory slight traces of impurities seem to prevent its formation, so it may not be a very good candidate for the interstellar dust. The yields of this substance have so far been too small to obtain any spectral or other physical information about it, except its high density (2.3 gm/cm^3); but it, too, may merit some consideration.

My point in mentioning these strange substances is really this: if the chemistry of well-studied material like water and carbon is so little understood that new forms are still being discovered under laboratory conditions, how many more surprises might await us in interstellar space, where time scales and physical conditions are very different from those in the chemical laboratory? We astronomers should keep our eyes open, from the infrared to the ultraviolet and beyond, in order to search out all possible observational clues which nature might give us about the composition of the interstellar dust. In the meantime let us not hang too many complex theories on assumed models which are not supported by observational evidence.

9. Remarks on the Interstellar Extinction Curve

ARTHUR D. CODE

Kitt Peak National Observatory

The average interstellar extinction curve shown in Figure 1 is based on ultraviolet measurements with the Orbiting Astronomical Observatory and ground-based spectrophotometry. The extinction is expressed in magnitudes and has been normalized to a (B-V) color excess of unity. The general characteristics of the interstellar extinction curve consist of a toe in the infrared, a nearly linear increase from λ 8000 to λ4000 Å, a kink or shoulder between λ 4000 and λ 3000, a striking peak around 2200 Å followed by a minimum near 1600 Å, and a rise to shorter wavelengths. The peak at 2200 angstroms was discovered by T. Stecher who subsequently suggested that it is due to graphite grains.

R. C. Bless and B. D. Savage are currently investigating the extinction curves for approximately 100 early type stars observed with OAO. It is clear from these data that the wavelength dependence of interstellar extinction exhibits large variations from object to object. It is also apparent that the variations are systematic. That is, in general it is possible to infer the shape of the entire extinction curve from the departures found within a restricted wavelength region. The dashed curve of Figure 1 shows the extinction curve found for the star σ Scorpii. In this case the far ultraviolet extinction is low, the shoulder between λ 4000 and λ 3000 Å is more pronounced, and the ratio of total to selective absorption in the visual is greater. All these variations seem to go along together in the material we have analyzed to date. The star σ Scorpii is surrounded by a dust cloud which is probably responsible for most of the extinction. The lower extinction shortward of 2000 Å appears to be imbedded in dust and nebulosity. ʘ Orionis, as first discussed by G. Carruthers, is an extreme case with very low extinction at shorter wavelengths. The analysis is much more difficult because the entire Trapizium is observed and significant contributions to the measured flux may come from the light scattered by the dust. If the entire deviation of the reddening curve in the ultraviolet were to be attributed to scattered light, however, it would require an albedo in excess of 95 percent. Since the extinction curve for ☉ Orionis is abnormal in the infrared and visual as well, it is most likely that the deviations are due to the nature of the interstellar grains.

We have attempted to fit the mean extinction curve with various grain models to see if the variations observed can be understood in a rational way. I am sure that a large variety of models could be found that would exhibit the wavelength dependence observed, but something that does work very well is a mixture of silicon carbide, graphite, and meteoric silicate particles. These constituents are currently believed to be possible condensation products during stellar mass loss. D. Gilra has carried out Mie calculations on such particles and finds that he can represent the observed curve very well with this three-component particle distribution. The silicon carbide is most effective in the wavelengths longer than 3000 Å. The graphite plays the major role in the 2000 Å region, while the silicates are responsible for the far ultraviolet extinction. If, now, the average particle size is increased, the extinction curve changes from that shown by the solid line in Figure 1 to that exhibited by the dashed line. These results

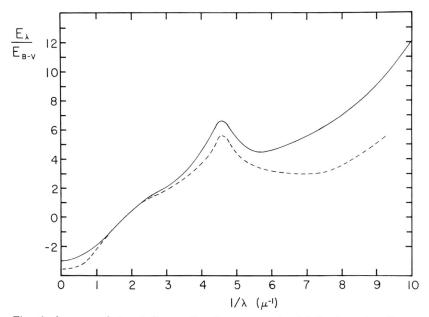

Fig. 1. Average interstellar extinction curve (solid line) and extinction curve for the star σ Scorpii (dashed line).

reinforce the idea that near hot early type stars the smaller particles are destroyed or removed from the vicinity. This particle distribution not only explains the observed wavelength dependence of extinction but gives the appropriate radar backscattering results for reflection nebulae. If, in addition, the grains are elongated to produce the observed polarization, they predict large polarization in the far ultraviolet.

There are some stars where the extinction is probably circumstellar and not interstellar. One of these stars, the nearest star Alpha Centauri, is apparently reddened but certainly not by the long path length.

In one sense this discussion of ultraviolet extinction is inappropriate in relation to dark nebulae. We have observed a number of dark clouds with the OAO and found that shortward of 1600 angstroms they appear bright. For example, in the Horsehead Nebula we have compared the dark and bright side. Shortward of 1600 angstroms the dark cloud appears brighter than the illuminated part of the nebula. This perhaps suggests that the albedo of the particles in this region is very high. A high albedo may extend to the region of Lyman alpha, since results by Blamont from OGO and preliminary OAO data indicate a possible galactic component of Lyman alpha. If the interstellar grains possess appreciable absorption, one would not expect any significant Lyman alpha flux because of the rather large number of scatterings of Lyman alpha photons by the neutral hydrogen.

In summary, the interstellar extinction in the ultraviolet is large, nonlinear, and shows relatively large systematic variation. Observational data of this kind should provide a very sensitive test for any of our ideas of what the interstellar grains may be.

Discussion

C. Townes: I gather from your remarks an implication that this brightness requires either an internal source of energy or a high albedo.

Code: This is a differential measurement. A more difficult thing is to measure how many photons you have. I would think that you wouldn't have to make it brighter than the star; if, for example, you had an opaque cloud around a star and you had complete scattering, then it would be as bright as that star at these wavelengths. All nebulae in the ultraviolet are essentially reflection nebulae and not emission nebulae. For example, it's rather like observing the corona of the sun at 5000 angstroms. Here the sun is too bright. But if you get a place with a lot of dust with a high albedo, the dusty region could be quite a bit brighter than the part that is just an excited nebula. Incidentally, this mixture of magnesium silicate does not give you an albedo of 1; it is more like 0.7 or so.

Townes: What about cladding of the grains? Can the grains be coated with a layer?

Code: If you make the carbon grains big, or if you put ice on them, the bump becomes very much wider and shifts to longer wavelengths. It's really quite sharp in all the observations, and there could only be a pretty thin coating. I know now, from what Gaustad said, that it isn't coated with ordinary ice, so if it is water-ice we'll have to use one of these super-ices. I had hoped that maybe one could put a thin layer of ice on that really wouldn't show, thin enough so that we don't see it until we get to the shorter wavelengths and maybe that would increase the albedo of these particles.

Townes: Would you say that whatever the material may be on the outside of these particles, this layer has to be pretty thin?

Code: I think you have to say that.

J. L. Greenstein: Have you tried to guess what paramagnetism, if any, the grains would have, if they are not made of something anisotropic, like carbon graphite?

Code: We haven't tried the alignment.

Greenstein: What is essential is to know how many and what valences or holes are available to produce paramagnetism. Is that correct, Dr. Townes?

Townes: I really don't know. I'm afraid the answer might be almost anything, depending on how the grains are formed.

P. G. Mezger: About two years ago we made a survey of HII regions of high surface brightness and, with the exception of Orion, in no cases could the exciting star be detected; which requires that the ionizing star must be in a cocoon of dust, which is possible only if the dust grains primarily scatter in the ultraviolet region and do not absorb.

Greenstein: It is rather interesting that if one takes seriously the observation that there are cool emitting regions in symbiotic objects or planetary nebulae like NGC 7027, you are forced into the same requirement of high albedo in the far ultraviolet for the dust. Or if you have a great deal of dust in the nuclei of active galaxies (to explain their infrared thermal emission) you must also have some way of getting the ionizing radiation to diffuse out through large optical depths.

F. J. Low: Perhaps John Gaustad or someone else would like to comment on what happened to the ices. It used to be certain that the interstellar grains had ice on them.

J. E. Gaustad: I don't think we know enough chemistry to say.

Townes: We know that the ices will condense out; the water and other gases are there, and the temperature sufficiently low in most places. What we don't know is how fast it comes off again.

N. Woolf: I have a comment about the emission of the cool stars and the idea of the silicates. One of the most disturbing features of the observations of the planetary nebulae Greenstein mentioned is that they appear to be completely different from the cool stars. Infrared emission from planetary nebulae resembles a black body rather well, whereas the emission in cool stars shows a very sharp peak near 10 microns.

A. Elvius: You mentioned that you see the dark clouds as bright in certain wavelengths, and you interpret this as a result of a high albedo. If so, then the extinction curves must be corrected for the scattered light.

Code: That is one of the major problems I was referring to when I said that to interpret Θ Orionis is a difficult problem. Not only do we have to match the stars but we have to do the transfer problem as well before we can construct any extinction curves.

T. Stecher: One of the difficulties with coating is that any good material becomes absorbent if you go far enough into the ultraviolet. What one really needs is some scattering, so you assume ice coatings; as you go farther into the ultraviolet, ice becomes an absorber and you just don't get enough extinction out there. We have difficulties making space observations in the ultraviolet; one must go to lithium fluoride, magnesium fluoride for mirror coatings, and they work. So it is quite puzzling what could produce the high scattering.

D. Harris: What one seems to need here is enough opacity in the material to get the high albedo. This is not a problem if we use some of the iron-oxygen compounds proposed recently by Huffman. Iron has very strong absorption in the ultraviolet so that the surface of the grain becomes essentially totally reflective because of an extremely large imaginary component in the refractive index.

10. Stars and Dark Nebulae

LEONARD V. KUHI

University of California, Berkeley

The subject matter under study here confines my remarks to those stars that are not sufficiently luminous to light up to any great extent the nebulosity in which they are found. However the same types of stars are also found in bright nebulosity with O and B stars; consequently I will make use of data derived from these sources as well as those obtained from dark clouds in order to describe the properties of the low-mass and intermediate-mass stars which constitute the "Orion Population."

The types of stars found in such nebulosity can be divided into several groups: T Tauri and T Tauri-like stars, irregular variables, flare stars, nondescript stars, and special objects such as FU Ori and R Mon which will not be discussed here. Their spectral and photometric properties can be described briefly as follows:

T Tauri stars. Spectral types range from late F to M. They are characterized by emission lines of H, Ca II, Fe II, He I, Ti II and other ionized metals; fluorescent lines of Fe I $\lambda 4063$, $\lambda 4132$; forbidden lines of [SII] $\lambda 6717, \lambda 6731$ and [OI] $\lambda 6300, \lambda 6363$. The underlying absorption spectrum when visible has considerably broader lines than would be expected for a normal star of the same spectral type (typically v sin i ≈ 50 km/sec). In addition the resonance line of Li I $\lambda 6708$ is very strong and leads to abundances comparable to that of the chondritic meteorites. These stars are irregular variables intimately connected with nebulosity, and their colors are also quite peculiar. They have large ultraviolet excesses (as large as 1.5 mag.), some indication of an overlying "blue continuum" which often obliterates the absorption spectrum, and also a strong infrared excess ascribed to the re-emission of absorbed stellar radiation by a circumstellar dust cloud (Low and Smith 1966). Only the visible-red region seems to be normal. In addition the emission lines often have P Cygni type profiles which indicate the outflow of material from their surfaces at rates as high as 6 x 10^{-7} M$_\odot$/yr. The weighted mean rate is about 4 x 10^{-8} M$_\odot$/yr (Kuhi 1964).

Irregular variables. Spectral types range from F to M. Some have H emission lines, but typically there is often no emission present at all. There is no large ultraviolet excess, but there is evidence for the presence of a shell and occasional P Cygni type emission profiles. The non-emission stars are about 1.5 times as numerous as the emission line stars. However in general these stars form a neglected group worthy of considerably more study.

Flare stars. Spectral types range from K to M. They are characterized by irregular rapid flares with timescales of minutes; that is, a risetime often less than one minute followed by essentially exponential decay. Between flares often only Hα is in emission, but during a flare there is a strong ultraviolet excess, H and Ca II emission lines, and a blue continuum as well. There is a subgroup "slow flares" in which the flares typically take 30 minutes to brighten and Hα appears after maximum light and persists for several days after minimum is reached. These stars are rather rare and are found only in regions where T Tauri stars are also present.

Nondescript stars. Spectral types range from F to M. They do not show emission or variability, but they constitute about 80 percent of the stars found in young clusters. They are a totally neglected group of stars because they don't do anything. However they clearly represent a later phase of pre-main sequence contraction, and more study is definitely in order.

Because of the peculiar colors, the precise location of these stars on the HR diagram is very uncertain. In addition the bolometric corrections now become quite large in view of the strong infrared radiation observed for many of these stars. Mendoza (1968) has used the $(V-R)_0$ colors as defined by the spectral type to correct for reddening by assuming that $(V-R)$ excess is caused only in interstellar extinction. He is then able to integrate under the UBVRIJHKLM photometry curve to obtain the total luminosity of individual T Tauri stars. These range from 4.9 $L_\odot$ for RW Aur to 50.0 $L_\odot$ for GW Ori for more normal T Tauri stars and as high as 828 $L_\odot$ for R Mon. The outstanding result is of course the extremely high luminosities which place the stars on convective tracks corresponding to 3 to 5 $M_\odot$ or even higher.

This is difficult to reconcile with previous estimates, which led to masses of about 1 to 2 $M_\odot$. One source of error which would lead to slightly higher luminosities (but only by 10 to 20 percent) is the contribution of Hα to the R band and the consequent over-correction for reddening. However the theoretical tracks do not consider the dynamical collapse phase, and hence it is probably premature to start worrying about the high masses derived from such conventional convective tracks. A more serious problem is the high luminosity itself, but this will be discussed by Low in the next chapter.

We can also get a cruder idea of where these objects lie by examining the color-magnitude diagrams of young clusters such as NGC 2264 and the Orion Nebula (Walker 1956, 1969). The stars of spectral type F and later basically lie above the zero-age main sequence (ZAMS) in a large fan-shaped area. Qualitatively their location above the ZAMS is as expected from stellar evolutionary calculations. Quantitatively the fanning-out behavior is not at all expected; nor is the location of stars *on the ZAMS and below the ZAMS*. It is clear that the usual broadband UBV colors are contaminated by emission lines (Smak 1964); however my own scanner observations indicate that the continuum colors (selected to avoid emission lines) are definitely peculiar and that as far as indicating their location on the color-magnitude diagram as implied by their *continuum* colors Walker's photometry is qualitatively correct.

The other types of stars and in particular the flare stars occupy the same part of the color-magnitude diagram. Flare stars, especially, often are found on and below the ZAMS, where according to theory they have no business being.

From the qualitative agreement with theoretical tracks we conclude that the vast majority of these stars appear to be still in the gravitational contraction phase of pre-main-sequence stellar evolution.

The best studied groups in this regard are the T Tauri stars and the flare stars. The properties of the flare stars have been determined largely through the efforts of Haro and Chavira (1968, 1969a, b) and their associates. They can best be summarized by looking at the results for flare stars in the Orion Nebula Region. The spectral types range from late G to early M, but most are around K. Many lie above the ZAMS but also many on and below it. All those lying below have $H\alpha$ in emission, and 44 out of 254 flare stars have emission lines even at low dispersion. Also about 25 percent are recognized as normal irregular variables of the T Tauri type with the flares superimposed on the larger scale variations. Not a single one of the Orion flare stars shows a more advanced M spectral type.

As different groups of young stars are studied an evolutionary pattern becomes clear. If the clusters or associations are ordered by age we find that the older the cluster the later the spectral type at which flare stars first appear. The following are examples:

Orion, NGC 2264	KO - M	$3 \times 10^5 - 10^6$ yr
Taurus dark cloud	KO - M5	10^6 (?)
Pleiades	K4 - M5	2×10^7
Hyades	MO - M6	4×10^8
Solar neighborhood	MO - M6	$> 5 \times 10^8$ (?)

In addition the fanning out of cluster sequences decreases with increasing age and the T Tauri-like characteristics are displaced to later and later spectral types. For example, flare stars and T Tauri stars appear together in very young clusters (such as NGC 2264 and the Taurus dark cloud) and often are indistinguishable from each other. However in older clusters only flare stars are seen; for example, there are no T Tauri-like stars in the Pleiades, but there are plenty of flare stars. In addition the ordering is one of a decrease in the amount of nebulosity and dark obscuring matter. No T Tauri stars (except for RW Aur) are found without the presence of nebulosity; nor are any flare stars of spectral type early K found without nebulosity. Finally when we compare the spectral characteristics of T Tauri stars and those of flares we find a general similarity; during a flare the ultraviolet and blue continua are strongly enhanced and the strength of the Balmer lines (especially Hα and Ca II, H, K) are greatly increased. The spectral development during a flare is beautifully illustrated by Kunkel (1967). Flare stars in general do not have the [OI] and [SII] lines found in T Tauri stars, but these arise from the nebulosity immediately surrounding the T Tauri star. Perhaps the flare stars do not have any such nebulosity because they never had very much to begin with or simply because they are incapable of retaining such nebulosity for some physical reason as yet not understood.

It seems quite likely that in the T Tauri stars we are seeing the results of a hyperactive chromosphere in which flares occur frequently over the entire surface of the star and provide a continual contamination of the continuum colors so that the stars appear much too bright in the ultraviolet as well as too blue for their spectral type. My scanner measurements indicate also a roughly defined sequence in which the T Tauri stars lie according to their emission activity: the stronger the emission line activity the farther they are located from the normal stars in a pseudo-two color diagram which plots ultraviolet continuum intensity versus a temperature index.

It is extremely tempting to draw the conclusion that what we are seeing is also an evolutionary sequence in which the activity decreases as the star gets older. Also this decline in activity is mirrored by the spectral type at which flares are first seen. Thus we might arrange the T Tauri and flare stars in order of increasing age as follows:

a) earliest : T Tauri, K, M flare stars
b) middle : residual UV; K5 - M flare stars
c) oldest : normal; M - flare stars

Since the scanner observations indicate a gap between the normal G-K stars and even the mildest T Tauri star on the UV-temperature plot, it is extremely likely that a residual excess ultraviolet and blue color remains in stars that have lost most if not all of their flare-like activity. This would presumably arise from the contributions from many minor flares, none of which is sufficient to affect the observed light output. It is even possible that the difficulty with the lower main sequence in the Pleiades may be due to this same residual excess flare-type continuum; that is, the M stars on the main sequence are too blue for their spectral type and should really be located somewhat further to the right. Hence there would be no requirement for noncoeval star formation, and so on, to explain the discrepancy. I am now in the process of observing such stars in the Pleiades and the Hyades (for comparison) to see if there is any truth to this speculation. Along a similar vein it would be very interesting to investigate the nonvariable and non-emission stars in the Taurus clouds and other young groups to see whether the presence of the ultraviolet excess could be used as an age criterion.

We might also ask where these stars are located with respect to the dark nebulae? In general whenever bright OB stars are present, the T Tauri and T Tauri-like stars are found in concentrations surrounding the OB stars. Also the nebulosity or obscuring matter must be fairly smoothly distributed; for example, T Tauri stars are not found in the presence of filaments or the dark concentrations of dust known as Bok's Globules. This anti-correlation refers only to the very dense globules with absorptions of the order of 10 magnitudes. However recent work by Bok (chapter 4, herein) and by Penston (1969) has revealed the presence of globules in Orion with lower absorption ($\sim$ 3 mag.) and hence lower particle density. Large numbers of T Tauri stars are found in Orion as well so that it seems that there may be some relationship between young stars and these less dense globules. What it is remains to be established. The flare stars in the youngest clusters follow much the same distribution.

In a dark cloud such as Taurus in which there are no OB stars present (the earliest is about B5) it is possible to look at their location in the cloud free from the confusion of HII regions and elephant trunks produced by the OB stars. Herbig and Peimbert (1966), using the method of star counts (used so extensively by Bok in his studies of the Milky Way) have been able to map out the most opaque parts of the Taurus dark cloud (that is, extinction of $\sim$1.5 magnitude with respect to the neighboring stars). The positions of $\sim$ 70 T Tauri and flare stars coincide extremely well with the densest parts of the cloud. In addition the surface density of T Tauri stars is proportional to the total absorption or opacity. In fact the number found is much larger than expected (by a factor of $\sim$3–5) if the rate of star formation is directly proportional to the local density (that is, to the first power of n). Also there are large regions in which no young stars have been found. Thus star formation is apparently favored in some parts of the cloud and not in others.

In addition Götz (1965) has found that the intensity of Hα emission in individual stars is also strongly correlated with the opacity of the cloud on which they are seen. This in turn implies some connection between the flare activity and the amount of dust from which the star formed.

Finally in this regard we should also mention the curious situation regarding the 21-cm observations of the Taurus dark cloud. Garzoli and Varsavsky (1966) have observed no great *excess or deficiency* of neutral H in those regions in which the T Tauri stars are concentrated as compared to those regions in which they are not; that is, typical density ranges of 1.1 to 2.9 $\times$ 10^{21} cm^{-2} were observed in both regions. Apparently the formation of stars in some parts of the cloud has not affected the distribution of atomic hydrogen at all. This is especially curious since the range in the dust concentration (as indicated by the obscuration) is quite marked.

In view of the aforementioned difficulty with high luminosity we should not forget that the very close association of T Tauri stars with the Taurus dark cloud (with space densities much higher than those of comparable field stars) was used to determine their age long before the existence of infrared observations beyond one micron. Even though the velocity dispersion of the stars is small (that is, 1–2 km/sec, which is similar to that of the HI in the cloud) it still places a limit of $\sim$5 x 10^6 yr as the maximum length of time that such an intimate association of stars with dust would survive. Thus it would be difficult to argue against the conclusion that these stars are very young objects indeed.

The bright nebulae reveal hundreds of young stars, often as many as the thousands estimated by Herbig for the Orion Nebula. In the Taurus dark cloud close to a hundred such stars are known. However the interesting question theoretically is: are there any regions in the sky in which only a few stars have formed, say fewer than 10 or even fewer than 100? The answer to this question is not clear. Certainly in the Taurus dark cloud the number is close to 100, but it is quite likely that there are easily many more stars hidden from our view.

In recent years Aveni and Hunter (1969) have put a great deal of effort into trying to answer this question. In particular they have studied a group of stars in the aggregate containing the T Tauri-like star BM And in a comet-like cloud nebulosity. Their color-magnitude diagram of only 8 stars (B8-F8e) suggests the presence of stars above the main sequence presumably in gravitational contraction. The mass of the stars is 20 to 30M$_\odot$ and they estimate the mass of the nebulosity to be $\sim$30 M$_\odot$ (assuming N$_{II}$ = 0.1 cm^{-3}, and a gas to dust ratio of 100:1). The total mass is therefore ~ 60 M$_\odot$. Hence this could be a case of star formation in a very small cloud. However membership was decided by spectroscopic parallaxes (distance $= 440 \pm 100$ pc) from low dispersion spectra. No proper radial velocity study has been made, and the results are not 100 percent convincing to me at least. Several other examples are NGC 7129 (< 200 M$_\odot$); NGC 7023 (< 150 M$_\odot$). BM And lies about 75 pc from the I Lac Association so that it could still be related to that association or the cloud may have been expelled from it at an earlier time. Clearly more study is needed to settle this question, since the usual arguments using the Jean's criterion for instability result in the formation of thousands of stars, not ten or a hundred, and hence the actual discovery of such groups will be crucially important in our understanding of star formation.

We can conclude from all this that stars are forming in dark clouds without the help of OB stars and that they are not very much bothered by our lack of understanding of the manner in which star formation actually takes place.

Discussion

Bart Bok: Where is there the best representative list of T Tauri stars?

Kuhi: In George Herbig's desk drawer. The next best is in the *Variable Star* Catalogue which lists them as RW or RWn. A list of brighter T Tauri stars is given in the review article by Herbig in volume one of *Advances in Astronomy and Astrophysics*.

T. K. Menon: Generally speaking, the nearest of these dark clouds seems to be also regions where observations of the molecular lines are not found to be very strong. One of the weakest OH absorption lines is in the direction of the Taurus source. Even in the case of Orion, the OH absorption lines are extremely weak. Where there are T Tauri stars, everything seems weakened. Somehow the molecules form much better in high density regions.

T. Hall: Has anyone observed the spectrum of one of the T Tauri stars as its brightness increases?

Kuhi: No, we haven't done that yet because they are so faint. The chances of observing them at just the right time are small. But the flare stars are much better. Namely, we get weaker flares going off in many stars as often as once an hour and stronger flares as often as once every four hours. So it is very easy, as Kunkel has done, to get continuous trailed spectra to show the spectrum before the flare and after the flare. Kunkel's spectra were of quite low dispersion, unfortunately, so that one couldn't do spectrophotometry on them, but it would be easy enough to do the same thing with high dispersion using the Lick 120-inch reflector. The main thing is the marked increase in H and Ca II emission line strength and the increased UV and blue continuum emission.

L. Aller: The flares of the type you are describing seem to be intrinsically different from typical solar flares, where the rise time is a matter of perhaps a few minutes, but they take 30 minutes or an hour or longer to decay. Hence, theoretical attempts to identify the two phenomena as one and the same thing encounter these time-scale difficulties. We cannot just take the results from solar physics and apply them uncritically to flares in these stars.

P. G. Mezger: Various lines of investigation appear to indicate that in O-star clusters and associations the low-mass stars are formed first and the most massive O-stars are formed last. Can you tell from your observations whether clouds that contain only T Tauri stars are younger than clouds that contain both T Tauri stars and O stars?

Kuhi: The methods of determining the ages of the Taurus dark cloud association and the OB associations are not sufficiently precise to say which group is younger. They come out essentially the same.

REFERENCES

Aveni, A. F., and Hunter, J. H., Jr. 1969, *A. J.* 75: 1021.

Garzoli, S. L., and Varsavsky, C. M. 1966, *Ap. J.* 145: 79.

Götz, W. 1965, *Veröff. Sternw. Sonneberg,* vol. 7, no. 1.

Haro, G. 1968, *Nebulae and Interstellar Matter,* ed. L. H. Aller and B. M. Middlehurst (Chicago: University of Chicago Press), p. 141.

Haro, G., and Chavira, E. 1969a, *Bol. Obs. Tonantzintla y Tacubaya* 5: 23.

————. 1969b, *ibid.* 5: 59.

Herbig, G. H., and Peimbert, M. 1966, *Trans. IAU,* 12B: 79.

Kuhi, L. V. 1964, *Ap. J.* 140: 1409.

Kunkel, W. E. 1967, Dissertation, University of Texas.

Low, F. J., and Smith, B. J. 1966, *Nature* 212: 675.

Mendoza V., E. E. 1968, *Ap. J.* 151: 977.

Penston, M. V. 1969, *M. N.* 144: 159.

Smak, J. 1964, *Ap. J.* 139: 1095.

Walker, M. F. 1956, *Ap. J. Suppl.* 2: 636.

————. 1969, *Ap. J.* 155: 447.

11. Galactic Infrared Sources

F. J. LOW

Lunar and Planetary Laboratory
University of Arizona
and
Department of Space Science
Rice University

Luminous galactic sources have been observed at wavelengths 5 to 100 times longer than the wavelengths at which the coldest of stars emit their energy. The existence of such high luminosity infrared objects is a great puzzle, with ramifications involving the formation and evolution of stars and extending to the problems of the composition and origin of interstellar matter; fortunately, the question of the radiative mechanism is answered convincingly by the observations. With only one important exception, all of the galactic objects that are now known to produce excess infrared emission can be understood in terms of a single radiative mechanism: thermal reradiation from dust which has been heated by high temperature radiation from one or more stars.

The galactic nucleus, the most luminous infrared source in our galaxy, is the only exception to this generalization; we have observed this compact source to emit in the far infrared about one percent of the luminosity of the entire galaxy. There is, however, observational evidence which appears to rule out the possibility that thermal reradiation from dust is the principal mechanism operating within the small volume occupied by the galactic nucleus. Arguments are even stronger against thermal reradiation from dust in the cases of extragalactic nuclei which are seen to exhibit infrared spectra quite similar to the galactic nucleus. Therefore, I would argue that the infrared source in the center of our galaxy is physically similar to the sources in the centers of other galaxies and is so different physically from the other galactic infrared sources that it should not be considered further in this discussion.

It is possible to divide the remaining bright infrared sources into three classes: (a) infrared stars, (b) infrared nebulae, and (c) H II regions. It is likely that additional bright sources of nonthermal radiation or intense line emission will be discovered. Indeed, the Crab Nebula radiates about 30 percent of its luminosity in the infrared by means of the

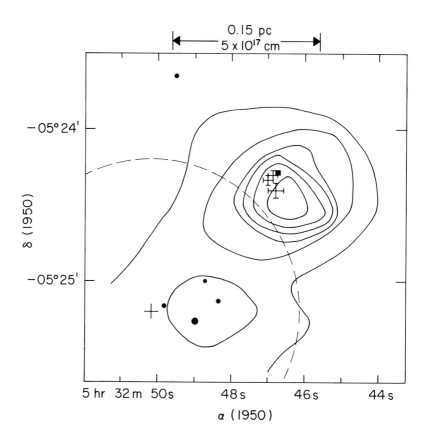

Fig. 1. Positions of infrared and radio sources in and near the trapezium region of the Orion Nebula. The cross near θ' (D) is the center of Orion A at 2 cm (Schraml and Metzger 1968); the dashed circle indicates the half power contour. The Ney-Allen infrared source, indicated here by a single 22 micron contour, is nearly coincident with the trapezium stars. The 22 micron contours to the northwest show the position and size of the Kleinmann-Low extended source. The Becklin-Neugebauer point source is indicated by a square of dimensions equal to the absolute positional uncertainty. Also included are the positions and their errors given by Raimond and Eliason (1967) for three small diameter OH sources. The 22 micron contours were taken from scans using a 15″ beam and are accurately located with respect to the Becklin-Neugebauer point source. The position of the point source (1950, $\alpha =$ 5h32m46.7s $\pm$ 0.1s; $\delta = -5°24'17'' \pm 1''$) was given by Becklin and Neugebauer (1968).

synchrotron process. Even if H II regions did not have strong infrared excesses, they would emit detectable infrared fluxes by free-free radiation. Here the discussion is restricted to known sources of excess infrared radiation.

All three classes of infrared sources are represented in a relatively nearby region close to the Orion nebula. Figure 1 shows the position of the radio source Orion A which is centered on the Orion nebula, an H II region excited by the four trapezium stars. An extended source of 10- and 20-micron radiation is nearly coincident with the center of this H II region. The extended source to the northwest is unique in that it emits no detectable optical or radio flux; it is a true infrared nebula. Presumably there are many more of these sources in the galaxy, but they are difficult to find since they emit almost exclusively in the far infrared. Just in front of the infrared nebula (or possibly just within its boundary) there is an example of an optically thick infrared star at a temperature of about $600°K$. The infrared star, which is close to a complex of OH sources, was discovered by E. E. Becklin and is denoted here as the Becklin-Neugebauer point source. The infrared nebula is denoted here as the Kleinmann-Low extended source, and the source coincident with the H II region is denoted as the Ney-Allen source.

The term "infrared star" has been used to denote a large but poorly defined class of stars which emit more infrared flux than expected. It now appears that many stars share this property to some degree, and an "exact" definition in terms of temperature or amount of excess infrared emission would be essentially arbitrary. Therefore, it seems logical to continue to use the term "infrared star" for any stellar system which clearly emits an infrared excess. If observations are carried out to wavelengths of 10 microns or longer, it is generally possible to distinguish between true infrared excesses and apparent excesses caused by interstellar extinction.

Table 1 is a list of 70 galactic objects observed to have substantial infrared excesses at 10 microns. This list was compiled by Susan Geisel (1970); she has used published spectroscopic information where available to divide the objects into several categories representing a wide range of luminosity and different stages of evolution. Most of these stars were found to possess low excitation emission lines (Fe II and [Fe III]) and line contours indicating large-scale mass loss. It should be noted that those stars marked by an asterisk were first observed in the infrared because of their low excitation emission lines or indications of mass loss. The color temperature, T_{K-N}, indicates the strength of the K-N excess and not the dust temperature unless the dust is optically thick.

These results imply a physical connection between the ejection of mass and the formation of grains in the resulting circumstellar envelope. Present evidence points to mass ejection as a prerequisite for the formation

TABLE 1

Stars with K-N Color Excesses of 0.5 Magnitude

(References Refer to Observations of FE II or FE III Emission)

Star	Ref	Sp	$T_{K-N}(°K)$	Star	Ref	Sp	$T_{K-N}(°K)$
Be-P Cygni Stars ($50 < L/L_⊙ < 10^4$)				**Cool Giants ($10^3 < L/L_⊙ < 10^4$)**			
*+61° 154	1	Beq	950	*R And	11	S6, 6e	990
*φ Per	1	B1pe	1900	S Per		M3ela	1150
*MWC 17	1	Pec	700	W Per		M5v	1320
*RR Tau	2	A2eII-III	980	R Lep		C7, 6e	1330
*HD 250550	2	A0e	910	W Aur		M3e	1040
*17 Lep	1	A2p	1200	VY CMa		cM3e	760
*Lk H α 208	2	B5-B9e	580	*ZZ CMi	6	gM6ep	1700
HD 45677	1	Bep	750	A0 Vir		M3e	1300
*HD 50091	2	Be	1200	WX Ser		M8e	1440
*Z CMa	1	Bep	880	MW Her		M9	1200
*HD 54858	2	Ae	900	CIT 11		M2-31	1750
*48 Lib	2	Bep	1500	DG Cyg		M7e	740
*HR 3135	3	B3p	1060	NWL Cyg		M6la	710
κ Dra		B7p	1500	μ Cep		M2ela	1850
*χ Oph	4	B3Vep	1600	**Symbiotic Stars ($L/L_⊙ \sim 10^4$)**			
*XX Oph	2	Bep	2420	*FR Sct	2	M2e	2100
*RY Sct	1	B0ep	740	R Aqr	6	M7e-Pec	1450
*+14° 3887	1	Pec	1730	**Novae and Nova-like Stars**			
β Lyr		Bep	2500	**($10^2 < L/L_⊙ < 10^6$)**			
*HD 190073	2	A0ep	860	FU Ori	12	cF5-G3la	1300
*P Cyg	5	B1eq	2350	η Car	1	Pec	540
*MWC 342	1	Be	850	*T CrB	2	gM3ep	1200
*MWC 349	1	Bep	840	Nova Ser (1970)	13		1600
*MWC 645	1	Bep	570	**Planetary Nebulae and Wolf-Rayet Stars**			
Ae-Fe-Ge Stars ($10^2 < L/L_⊙ < 10^4$)				**($10^2 < L/L_⊙ < 10^4$)**			
*AB Aur	2	A0ep	1050	IC 418			750
*HK Ori	1	A4ep	840	NGC 6543			800
T Ori		A3e	1000	NGC 6572			500
V380 Ori	2	A+neb.	1000	+30° 3639			600
*W Ser	2	cG2e	1480	HD 192163			1950
				NGC 7027	14		850
T Tauri Stars ($25 < L/L_⊙ < 10^3$)				**Optically Thick Infrared Stars**			
T Tau	6	dG5e	820	**($L/L_⊙ \sim 10^3$)**			
CO Ori		gGe	1150	Becklin's Object			720
GW Ori		dK3e	990	IRC + 10216			550
R Mon	2	A-Fpe	810				
*RU Lup	7	G5±e	880				
R CrA	2	Fpe	940				
T CrA		F0e	750				
BM And		F8e	1250				
Hydrogen-poor Stars ($L/L_⊙ \sim 10^3$)							
*HD 30353	8	G0ep	1450				
Su Tau		G0ep	860				
R CrB	2	cFpep	1000				
RY Sgr	9	G0ep	860				
υ Sgr	10	Apep	1060				

* Stars first observed in infrared because of low excitation emission lines or indications of mass loss.
1 Merrill and Burwell 1933, 1943, 1949.
2 Wackerling 1970.
3 Jaschek, Jaschek, and Malaroda 1969.
4 Cleminshaw 1936.
5 Beals 1955.
6 Merrill 1927
7 Merrill 1942.
8 Bidelman 1950.
9 Feast 1969.
10 Greenstein and Adams 1947.
11 Merrill 1947.
12 Herbig 1966.
13 Burkhead, Seeds and Lee 1970.
14 Aller, Bowen and Minkowski 1955.

and maintenance of these circumstellar dust envelopes. Not only do we have the circumstantial evidence of Table 1, where mass loss is seen to accompany the infrared excess at 10 microns, but we must consider that radiation pressure on the particles tends to overcome gravitational attraction. Even in the case of the solar system 0.1 micron diameter particles are not gravitationally bound. The ratio of solar gravitational force to the force exerted by solar radiation is (1.7×19^4) $a\rho$ where a is the diameter of the small black particle in centimeters and ρ is the density. Gravitational attraction is proportional to the mass of the star, whereas the radiation pressure is proportional to the star's luminosity. All of the infrared objects observed so far are much more luminous than the Sun, but their masses cannot exceed the mass of the Sun by similar factors: therefore, unless the particles are very large they will be rapidly ejected from the circumstellar envelopes. Unless new dust is formed to replace the dust driven outward by radiation pressure we would not expect to see such high luminosity systems with circumstellar shells of nearly constant brightness and temperature. Obviously, this question of the rate of formation of circumstellar dust and its ejection into the interstellar medium is fundamental and must be investigated further.

Low, Johnson, Kleinmann, Latham, and Geisel (1970) have studied six infrared stars in some detail, using both spectroscopic and photometric data. Figure 2 shows the normalized spectral energy distributions of these stars over the wavelength interval where most of their flux is emitted. It should be possible to separate the observed spectral distribution into two components: (a) radiation from the central star transmitted through the circumstellar envelope and (b) thermal reradiation emitted by the dust in the circumstellar envelope. The assumption must be made that the dust is heated only by radiation from the central star whose temperature is deduced from spectral information. This separation was carried out for R Mon, T Tau, and VY CMa. For both HD 45677 and Becklin's Object the circumstellar dust is optically thick at visible wavelengths so no information is available about the temperature of the central stars. NML Cyg appears to be intrinsically identical to VY CMa in all respects, but it is located behind a dense interstellar cloud which obscures its optical emission. Rather remarkable similarities were found to exist between the thermal reradiation spectra of these six objects. Table 2 summarizes the physical properties deduced from this study. In each case most of the infrared radiation is emitted by a dust shell at temperatures near $600°$K.

Additional information about the dust can be obtained by comparing the circumstellar extinction curves to normal interstellar extinction curves. Here the results indicate that much of the circumstellar dust is similar to interstellar dust but that larger particles are also present. Particle size

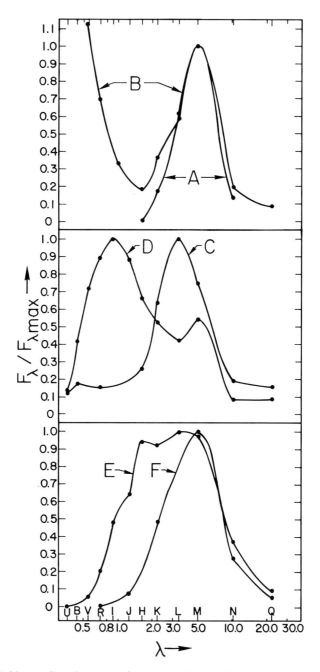

Fig. 2. Normalized spectral energy distributions of six infrared stars, (A) Becklin's object (Becklin-Neugebauer point source), (B) HD 45677, (C) R Mon, (D) T Tau, (E) VY CMa, (F) NML Cyg.

TABLE 2

Physical Properties

	Becklin's Object	HD45677 Companion	HD45677 IR Star	R Mon	R Mon Shell	T Tau	T Tau Shell	VY CMa	VY CMa Shell	NML Cyg Observed	NML Cyg Intrinsic
Sp	—	B3(V)	—	(G5)	—	KI	—	M6-7Ia	—	M6-7Ia	M6-7Ia
Distance (pc)	500	750	750	700	700	150	150	400	400	520	520
Flux ($\times 10^{-15}$ W/cm^2)	13	—	13	3.0	2.8	2.2	1.2	800	500	400	450
$L/L_\odot$	1000	1000	2200	460	430	15	8.5	30,000	20,000	—	30,000
T Shell (°K)	600	—	580	—	850	—	580	—	580	—	580
Ang. Dia. (")	0.05	—	0.06	0.013	0.013	0.024	0.018	0.458	0.362	—	0.343
Lin. Dia. (a.u.)	14	—	23	4.8	4.6	2.0	1.4	90	73	—	90
A_V (mag)	—	—	—	~ 4	—	2.5	—	2.5	—	9.5	2.5
Mass (gm)	—	—	—	10^{27}	—	—	5×10^{24}	—	2.5×10^{28}	—	2.5×10^{28}

effects can also be seen in the extremely narrow shape of the thermal reradiation spectra.

When a quantitative understanding of the formation of these circum-stellar shells has been reached it may be possible to estimate what contributions they make to the solid component of the interstellar medium. It seems entirely possible that the origin of interstellar dust has been found.

When Low and Smith (1966) first proposed the thermal reradiation model for the infrared emission of R Mon it was emphasized that a pre-planetary system of about one solar mass might be expected to have very similar properties. This gave support for the hypothesis that T Tauri-like objects are protostars. Now there are two objections to this simple picture: (a) radiation pressure is rapidly dissipating the solid particles from the circumstellar nebula which is maintained by mass ejection from the star, and (b) the luminosities of these objects, including the very large infrared contribution, may be too high to be supported entirely by gravitational collapse over the periods which are indicated by the frequency of their occurrence.

It may be that one-solar-mass protostars are infrared sources surrounded by an opaque cloud of dust but that their luminosity remains too low for them to be detected at present levels of sensitivity. Perhaps the Bok globules, which are not yet detected in the infrared, are still the most likely candidates for this early stage of stellar evolution.

Because it is the only object of its kind, the Kleinmann-Low extended source has been observed over the entire range of infrared wavelengths from 5 microns to 100 microns. From 25 to 300 microns the observations were carried out by H. H. Aumann and the author, using a 12-inch diameter far infrared telescope operated in a jet aircraft to overcome the opacity of the Earth's lower atmosphere. Figure 3 shows these results along with groundbased observations. The passbands of the three wideband filter systems used in the airborne telescope are indicated at the top of the figure by arrows. The dark portion of the curve is the result of a model constructed to fit the observed fluxes in the three wideband filters. The 10 and 22 micron groundbased observations fit this model quite well, but at 5 microns there may be more radiation than the model predicts. In constructing this model Aumann (1970) has taken into account the size of the source and its observed variation with wavelength. The 22 micron contours shown in Figure 1 were obtained by Kleinmann and Low. The source grows larger with wavelength and becomes less dense to its own radiation.

As a result of these studies we can give the total luminosity as 10^5 $L_\odot$ and the minimum mass, including dust and gas, at about 200 $M_\odot$ The size of the object is approximately 7×10^4 A. U., and it is probably expand-

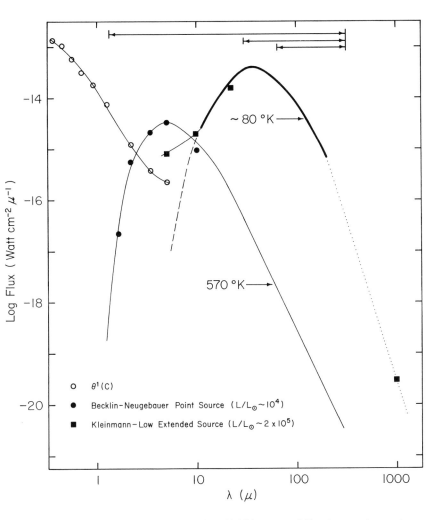

Fig. 3. Log F (ν) versus Log ν for θ' (C), one of the trapezium stars, the Becklin-Neugebauer point source and the Kleinmann-Low extended source. The observation at 1000 microns was made using the 36-foot millimeter wave telescope operated by the National Radio Astronomy Observatory.

ing under its own radiation pressure. Figure 4 shows the variation of dust temperature with distance calculated from the radiative transfer model of Aumann. The temperature of the dust excludes ices as major constituents, and Aumann has found that the far infrared radiative efficiency of pure graphite grains is far too low to produce the observed fluxes. So-called impure graphite particles were used in the model calculations. The optical depth at optical wavelengths is computed to be about 150.

It is interesting to speculate about the nature of this singular object. If the Orion nebula itself were compressed back to its proto-cluster stage of evolution, its properties would seem to match those of the Kleinmann-Low object, its younger neighbor.

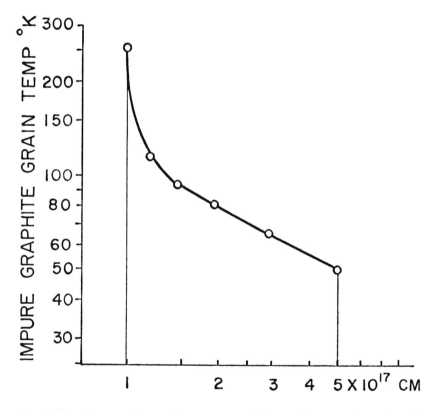

Fig. 4. The temperature of impure graphite grains as a function of distance from the center of the Kleinmann-Low extended source, based on the model of Aumann (1970).

Ney and Allen (1969) found an extended source almost coincident with the trapezium stars at the center of the radio source Orion A. Kleinmann has shown that the twin H II region M17, which is quite similar to Orion A, has extended infrared emission quite similar to that found by Ney and Allen. A number of planetary nebulae and other H II regions such as M8 should be included in this class of objects (Gillett, Low and Stein 1967; Gillett and Stein 1970; Woolf 1969).

It appears that all H II regions share this infrared phenomenon. Generally, the infrared is emitted by small diameter dust particles and the dust content of the nebula is not necessarily higher than in unionized interstellar clouds. The surface brightness is much lower than the color temperature and the 10 micron contours match the radio contours

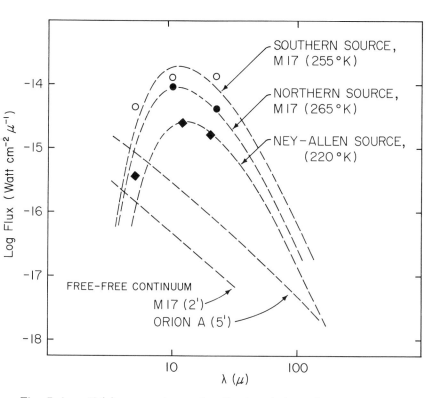

Fig. 5. Log F (λ) versus Log λ for the two infrared sources in M 17 and for the Ney-Allen source in the Orion Nebula. Calculated free-free continua are also shown.

(Fig. 6). This is consistent with optically thin dust in radiative equilibrium with the surrounding plasma. It is surprising, of course, that a large fraction of the total luminosity of the nebula is transferred to the dust and emitted in the infrared.

The grains are probably frozen into the plasma by Coulomb forces which greatly retards their motion through the plasma. It is not clear whether we are seeing the original interstellar dust present in the gas before it was ionized or whether the dust is formed *in situ* after the ionization. In any case dust grains in an ionized cloud may be quite unlike those in a cold neutral cloud. Further studies of the infrared emission from optically thin sources should better define the physical properties of the dust.

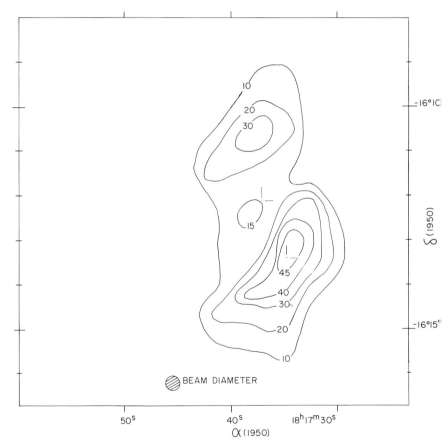

Fig. 6. Contours of M 17 from scans made by D. E. Kleinmann. The agreement with published radio contours is excellent.

At least three classes of luminous infrared sources are now known to exist in our galaxy. Thermal reradiation from dust heated by one or more luminous stars serves as an adequate radiative mechanism in all these objects. However, the origin or formation, composition and ultimate disposition of the solid particles are still very much in question. Considerable evidence favors the view that the dust is rapidly condensed out of ejected matter and is ultimately dispersed into the interstellar medium by radiation pressure. The infrared nebula in Orion is probably an expanding cluster of protostars; however, it is doubtful that individual infrared stars are true examples of protostars. Luminous infrared sources are now expected in all H II regions.

As a footnote, added because of very recent observations, it should be noted that a fourth class of infrared source may have been found. At 100 microns there are two intense discrete sources within one degree of the galactic nucleus. The brightest of these sources is brighter than the nucleus itself and may be more luminous; however, the spectrum appears different from anything observed previously. There are several H II regions nearby which may be related to the infrared sources; one of these is the highly anomalous region discussed by Dr. N. Deiter in these proceedings.

Discussion

Hugh Johnson: When you observed alpha Sco, did you try to separate the two components? Struve and Swings discovered a very peculiar nebula around the dwarf B4 component. This nebula has a unique spectrum which is composed mostly of FeII emission. It might be interesting if you could observe that nebula separately from the cool star.

Low: If it's a few seconds of arc I'm sure it can be done.

Johnson: It is a few seconds.

C. Pecker: As soon as you are able to give a model which takes into account the fact that the cloud is partially composed of dust, of which the properties can a priori be height dependent, you can conclude something about these properties and their depth-dependence by comparison with your observed energy distributions, which depart slightly from black-body distributions. Also, you have mentioned that in your cloud, dirty ice was a possibility; could you elaborate a little bit this point?

Low: In the case of the Orion infrared nebula, where we had tried to deduce the properties of the dust from a model which produces the observed spectral and spatial distributions of energy, the result is that so-called "dirty-ice" would be an excellent possibility except for the temperatures which are probably too high. The other infrared sources are far too hot for ice.

Pecker; So the departure from black-body conditions is what gives it.
Low: True.

R. Weymann: I'd like to ask you about your comment that the conventional idea of gravitational contraction isn't sufficient to account for the energy. *Low:* What I should have said perhaps is that you can do it if you have enough mass; gravitational contraction is not adequate unless the masses of these objects are high.

Weymann: But suppose you took just one solar mass; that gives you a time scale of something like 10^5 solar years.

Low: In the Hayaski treatment of the formation of a one solar-mass star, the luminosity reaches 10^3 $L_\odot$ but lasts for too short a time to be observed. Other treatments of this problem distribute the same gravitational energy over a longer time period, but since the total energy supply remains the same, the peak luminosity is then too low to match the observations. (For some recent results, see Larson, M.N. 145, 271. Ed.)

Weymann: What can you say about the time scales, on some kind of statistical argument?

Low: This question needs to be studied as the sample of objects grows.

A. Poveda: From your data, it appears that you can classify the sources into two groups: objects which are not very luminous, like T Tauri, in which case there is no problem with the lifetimes, and objects having more than 10,000 times the solar luminosity. Probably in the latter case what you have is a very young cluster of massive stars still embedded in a dense cloud. In support of this interpretation I would like to point out that the Trapezium in Orion in its early days may have looked similar to the bright objects that you have described. A final remark I wish to make has to do with the lithium problem. The Li abundances observed in T Tauri stars and related objects can be interpreted as the result of the spallation of the CNO nuclei by an intense flux of corpuscular radiation. When one works out the energetics of the problem, taking into account efficiencies of the order of 10 percent for the accelerating mechanism, one finds an enormous flux of thermal radiation which appears in the infrared as an excess radiation comparable to those observed in objects like T Tauri. In the latter case an opaque circumstellar cloud is not required.

G. Burbidge: That doesn't solve the problem.

J. L. Greenstein: What Poveda says has a good deal of merit, but it is perhaps an oversimplification to say that one has a simple thermal process. The background of astrophysical theory in this area isn't zero. The radiation transfer problem in the spherically-symmetric case has been solved. If you assume a simple dependence of opacity on density, the solutions (given by Kosyrev and by Chandeasekhar, around 1930) show both an enormous infrared and ultraviolet excess. The extreme limb darkening in an object with a very extended envelope results that when you look at the center you see a very hot star, while at the limb you see a very cool thing; the flux is not describable by a unique temperature. The model you used was of a high singularity and temperature peak in the center. There are many symbiotic objects in which it seems that objects supposed to be composite are in fact single objects with a hot center and a cool common envelope.

Low: Are you referring to HD 45677, where we consider it to consist of an optically thick infrared star and a B-star?

Greenstein: Yes, the point is that there is no M star in HD 45677. I looked for it, and so has our infrared group using moderately good resolution, and there is no trace of bands.

Low: In my model the reason that no spectral contribution from the infrared star is seen is that the dust is optically thick at short wavelengths. This is true in Becklin's object and in IRC +10216.

Greenstein: No bands?

Low: It is unfortunate that in these cases, optically thick infrared stars and nebulae, the information normally conveyed by optical spectroscopy is lost.

Greenstein: The total energy that one has to worry about has a large unknown component perhaps not only gravitational but also magnetic. I think that what Poveda says is very likely to be true. It takes about 600 million volts to produce a single lithium atom, and most of this has to go out as gamma rays or soft cosmic rays. If you assume equipartition, that is, that the magnetic and gravitational field are the same, you gain only factors of 2, and that's not going to work; you need factors of 10 or 100 for the total energy source.

Low: I also agree that an additional energy source must be found for many of these objects if they are pre-main sequence.

C. Townes: Is there no difficulty with rate of loss of dust particles for a 1 solar mass star? Because, if you put 10^{-3} or 10^{-5} solar mass in a dust cloud which is moving outward as rapidly as you indicate, I suppose the star's mass would be dissipated in too short a time unless it initially has a very high mass. Once the dust cloud motion implies a star of very large mass, then the gravitational energy would appear to be an adequate energy source and perhaps no new assumption about its origin is needed.

J. Hall: People keep saying, "When Frank Low builds a more efficient detector . . ." and so on. How efficient are they now?

Low: For ground-based broad band photometry at 10 and 22 microns, the detectors are already as good as they need to be. The photon noise limit has been reached; the photons emitted by the telescope mirrors produce this noise, and it is clearly not a question of a better site or a more efficient detector. For the airplane telescope or for more advanced systems, we still do need better detectors because the background can be much lower than from the ground. For narrow band work or spectroscopy, which is the great hope for the future, the answer is less clear. Fourier spectroscopy results in large backgrounds on the detector, and we cannot say which technique will ultimately prove to be the most powerful.

REFERENCES

Aller, L. H., Bowen, I. S., and Minkowski, R. 1955, *Ap. J.* 122: 62.

Aumann, H. H. 1970, unpublished Ph. D. dissertation, Rice University.

Beals, C. S. 1955, *Pub. Dominion Astrophys. Obs.* 9: 1.

Bidelman, W. P. 1950, *Ap. J.* 11: 333.

Burkehead, M. S., Seeds, M. A., and Lees, V. J. 1970, *IAU Circ.* no. 2220.

Cleminshaw, C. H. 1936, *Ap. J.* 83: 487.

Feast, M. W. 1969, in *Non-Periodic Phenomena in Variable Stars,* ed. L. Derek (Budapest: Academis Press).

Geisel, S. L. 1970, *Ap. J.* (*Letters*) 161: L105.

Gillett, F. C., Low, F. J., and Stein, W. A. 1967, *Ap. J.* (*Letters*) 149: L97.

Gillett, F. C., and Stein, W. A. 1970, *Ap. J.* 159: 817.

Greenstein, J. L., and Adams, W. S. 1947, *Ap. J.* 106: 339.

Herbig, G. H. 1966, in *Vistas in Astronomy,* ed. A. Beer (London: Pergamon Press).

Jaschek, M., Jaschek, C., and Malroda, S. 1969, *Astron. and Astrophys.* 3: 485.

Low, F. J., and Smith, B. J. 1966, *Nature* 212: 675.

Merrill, P. W. 1927, *Ap. J.* 65: 286.

——. 1942, *Pub. A. S. P.* 53: 342.

——. 1947, *Ap. J.* 106: 274.

Merrill, P. W., and Burwell, C. G. 1933, *Ap. J.* 78: 87.

——. 1943, *Ap. J.* 98: 153.

——. 1949, *Ap. J.* 110: 387.

Ney, E. P., and Allen, D. A. 1969, *Ap. J.* (*Letters*) 155: L193.

Wackerling, L. R. 1970, *Mem. R. A. S.* 73: 153.

12. Models of Interstellar Clouds

GEORGE B. FIELD

University of California, Berkeley

Because much of the work to be described here depends on radio observations, it is appropriate to recall Bart Bok's role as one of the founders of the National Radio Astronomy Observatory.

Dust, calcium, and neutral hydrogen are distributed in a nonuniform manner. Calcium and hydrogen are correlated, but the correlation with dust is a matter of controversy. Here we consider the distribution of hydrogen from a physical standpoint and comment on implications for sodium, calcium, and dust.

Although nonuniformity appears on every scale from less than a parsec to more than a kiloparsec, here we consider particularly the clumpiness that appears on a scale of a few parsecs. The virial theorem indicates that clumps of gas with dimensions of a few parsecs and densities of a few atoms per cubic centimeter cannot be gravitationally bound; the internal pressure (kinetic and turbulent) is too large. If no other forces were involved, these clouds would expand and disappear in 10^7 years.

There are three possibilities for confining the gas in clouds (Spitzer, 1968): (i) dynamic pressure (ρv^2) associated with the impact of other clouds (Kahn and Dyson, 1965); (ii) magnetic stresses ($B^2/8\pi$) working in cooperation with the galactic gravitational field (Parker, 1966); and (iii) gas pressure (p) in an external medium of low density (Spitzer, 1951). Each of these possibilities has been studied relatively independently of the others, but each may play a role under various circumstances.

The possibility of dynamic confinement is best discussed within the framework of a recent study of a collision between two clouds (Stone, 1970). It is clear from the observations of calcium components that clouds move with an r.m.s. velocity of about 10 km/sec. It is difficult to imagine how they can avoid colliding with each other. As the mean free path can be estimated as 100 parsecs from the observation that there are about 10 calcium components per kiloparsec, the mean time between collisions is about 10^7 years. When a collision occurs with a relative velocity about 10 km/sec, a shock wave propagates into each cloud, since the sound speed corresponding to $100°$K is only 1 km/sec. These shocks slow the incoming gas and, because of rapid cooling behind the shock, compress

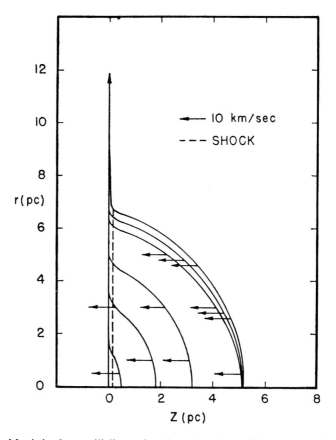

Fig. 1. Model of a colliding cloud at $t = 8 \times 10^5$ years, when the shock has propagated ⅔ of the way through the cloud. The effect of another cloud moving to the right has been replaced by a rigid wall at $z = 0$. The gas which has passed through the shock (dashed line) is compressed about 100 times. The high pressure causes an expansion to the sides which results in the loss of 6% of the mass. (From Stone, 1970)

the gas to a thin layer having about 100 times the original density, some $10^3 cm^{-3}$. This layer later expands at the sound speed, about 1 km/sec, taking about 10^7 years to attain a radius of 10 parsecs. The details of the compression and expansion phases are indicated in Figures 1 and 2.

The coincidence of 10^7 years for both the collision and the expansion time suggests a model in which clouds are prevented from expanding beyond 10 parsecs by collisions and the associated dynamic pressure (Kahn and Dyson, 1965). A problem with this view is that statistically some clouds will manage to avoid a collision for two or three times the mean collision time and will therefore be able to expand to 20 or 30 parsecs to a density below 1 cm^{-3}. At this point they no longer have higher density than the average, and they have ceased to exist as distinct clouds. This picture therefore requires means of forming new clouds, such as the mechanisms (ii) and (iii).

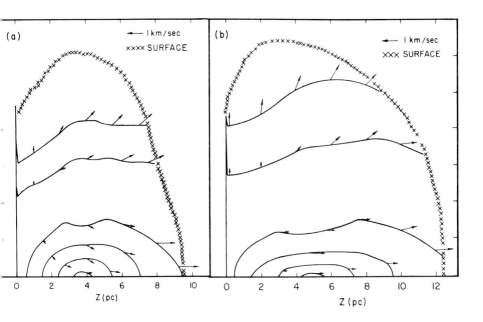

Fig. 2. Model at t $=$ 10^6 years and 1.2 $\times$ 10^7 years. An expansion wave has entered the cloud and set the gas into outward motion. During this phase the external pressure begins to retard the expansion. The expansion velocity may account for the observed sodium line widths of $\sim$ 1 km/sec. (From Stone, 1970)

    The model indicates that those clouds participating in a collision
should be very dense, cold, and flattened. Thus, in the most highly compressed state, the mean density is $10^3 cm^{-3}$; but this decreases with time
in a calculable manner as the cloud expands. This model therefore predicts
a rather definite distribution of cloud densities, ranging up to $10^3 cm^{-3}$.
It also predicts that many clouds should be expanding with velocities about
1 km/sec; this may be observed.
    Turning to possibility (ii), the argument here is that gravity and
magnetic field can cooperate to confine a cloud as in Figure 3. Here the
gas is trapped in a magnetic well. It cannot move upward along the
magnetic field because of the galactic gravitational field; hydrostatic
equilibrium along each line of force gives it a scale height which is $(100/z)$
pc for a cloud temperature of $100°K$. Neither can it move horizontally
without expending energy. To see why, imagine the extreme case that the
gas in adjacent clouds expanded to fill the lines of force uniformly in the
horizontal direction. Then the field would be weighted equally everywhere and would be horizontal. Such a configuration has larger field
strength and hence higher magnetic energy, so that force must be exerted
to reach it. It appears that the configuration of Figure 3 is a stable one
which can account for the confinement of clouds.
    This picture depends on the possibility of a cold $(\sim 100°K)$ com-
ponent of HI, since the scale height in the well is proportional to T.
Otherwise the vertical extent of the clumps would be too great for ordinary

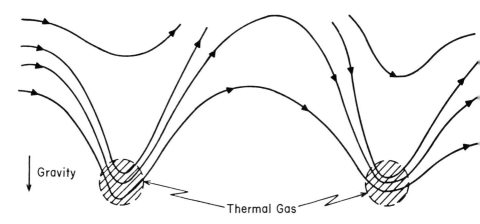

Fig. 3. Magnetic wells and confined clouds in Parker's model in the
spiral arm where a cold dense phase is possible. Similar wells can
form in the interarm region, but may not have cold gas in them.
(From Parker, 1966)

clouds. Hence magnetic confinement must be considered in conjunction with the thermal state of the gas, which we consider below.

Magnetic confinement would have certain observational consequences. The polarization vectors of stars shining through a cloud should rotate systematically from one side of the cloud to the other. The edges of the clouds should be sharp and should be correlated with the direction of the polarization vectors. The vertical extent depends upon the local gravity and should therefore decrease with the height of the cloud as gravity increases.

Alternative (iii) is based on recent studies of heating by cosmic rays and X-rays (Spitzer and Scott, 1969; Goldsmith, Habing and Field, 1969; Hjellming, Gordon and Gordon, 1969; Silk and Werner, 1969), which indicate that any residual gas between clouds will be hot and therefore have a pressure contributing to the confinement of clouds. The cosmic-ray flux is not known in the energy range of interest (several MeV), but if there are the equivalent of 0.04 eV/cm^3 2 MeV protons present, the balance of cosmic-ray heating and cooling by inelastic collisions yields curves like those of Figure 4. (In these studies, H$_2$ has been neglected. Recent work by Hollenbach, Werner and Salpeter suggests that H$_2$/H could be as much as 10^{-3} in normal clouds. This would have some effect on cooling rates.) At high densities, T is held down to $\sim 100°$K by processes involving O atoms and C, Si, and Fe ions; the value of the equilibrium temperature depends on the abundances. If $n_H < 0.2$ cm^{-3}, the temperature must rise to compensate the reduced collision frequency, and does so until Lyman-α excitation becomes effective at $\sim 10^4°$K (independent of the heavy-element abundances). The corresponding gas pressure is shown in Figure 5.

Disturbances which take the gas away from the curve where the net heat loss vanishes (L = 0) usually tend to relax back to that curve. If the disturbances are of small scale (a few parsecs), the relaxation occurs at constant pressure. Perturbations of high density therefore have lowered temperature, and in the vicinity of the rising branches of the pressure curve, lie in the domain L<0. Therefore in these regions the gas heats up and expands back to the density on the equilibrium curve; the time scale for this is 10^7 years in the hot gas and 10^5 years in the cool gas. If the perturbation is near the descending branch, it is in the domain L>0, and therefore cools and compresses further on a time scale of 10^6 years. This thermal instability may be relevant for cloud formation, in which the final state is one with two phases present — a cold dense phase (clouds) in pressure equilibrium with a hot rarefied phase (intercloud medium (Field, 1965). At first sight it seems unlikely that such can occur, because heat will tend to be conducted from the hot to the cold gas. However, it has been shown (Penston and Brown, 1970) that this heat flow is confined to a boundary layer some 0.04 pc thick, in which the heat is conducted from the outer parts of the layer (where $L<0$ from Figure 5) to the inner parts (where $L>0$).

We see that the cool phase cannot exist below $p_{min} \simeq 10^2 cm^{-3} {}^\circ K$ and that the hot phase cannot exist above $\simeq 10^3 cm^{-3} {}^\circ K$ if the abundances are solar (the critical pressures have been recently revised by additional cooling mechanisms). Wherever the pressure tends to exceed $\sim 10^3$, clouds must form — "a phase transition occurs." One place where this may occur is in the magnetic wells discussed above, where hydrostatic balance along the lines of force means that the pressure must equal the weight of the gas above. If the latter exceeds p_{max}, clouds must form. Within the clouds, the density will decrease upward with a scale height of a few parsecs, but before the pressure has fallen to p_{min} at $n_H \simeq 1$ cm^{-3}, there should be a sharp (~ 0.04 pc) transition to hot gas at a much lower density.

According to one model (Field, Goldsmith, and Habing, 1969), about ¾ of the gas in a spiral arm is in clouds and the rest in the intercloud medium. The clouds contribute most of the 21-cm emission and all of the absorption. Nevertheless, the intercloud medium should be visible as a weak, broad, 21-cm feature, since it is only 10 percent ionized. Some authors (Clark, 1965; Mebold, 1969; Radhakrishnan and Murray, 1969), have interpreted 21-cm observations in support of such an intercloud medium, but the evidence may not support temperatures for this phase as high as required theoretically if solar abundances apply ($>8000^\circ K$).

Recently Peter Meszaros and I have studied the effects which accretion of interstellar atoms and ions on dust grains might have on this picture. Since only heavy elements will stick to the grains, the clouds are gradually scoured of the species which they require to cool effectively, and the clouds will heat up in proportion to their age (defined as the time since accretion began). This effect is helpful in explaining the variety of cloud temperatures observed (25-$150^\circ K$) as well as the relative deficiency of calcium with respect to sodium, since Ca^{++} depletes faster than Na^+ because its higher charge attracts it more to the negatively-charged grains.

Figure 4 shows the effects of depleting the heavy elements by the factors indicated. One can calculate the time to reach a point in this diagram if a relation between ρ and T is assumed. For a small cloud, this relation is simply that p=constant=external pressure, since depletion is very slow in the intercloud medium, and its temperature does not change. In Figure 5 we see the results of evolution at various pressures. Note that if $p = 10^3 cm^{-3} {}^\circ K$ for example, a critical point is reached at n = 3 cm^{-3}, T = $330^\circ K$ when further depletion would require an increase in pressure.

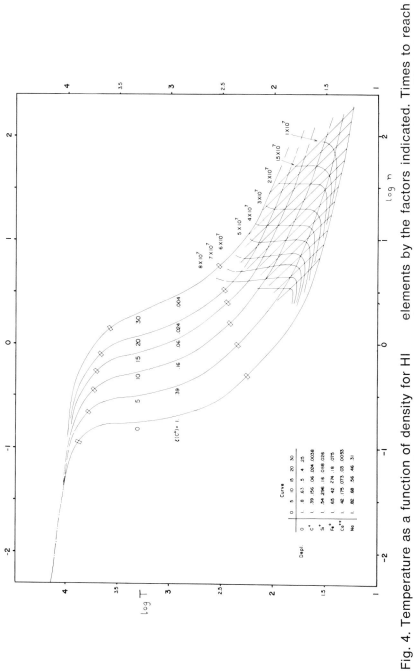

Fig. 4. Temperature as a function of density for HI in thermal equilibrium and heated by cosmic rays. The various curves refer to depletion of the heavy elements by the factors indicated. Times to reach these at constant pressure are shown. (Calculations in Figs. 4, 5, and 6 by P. Meszaros at Berkeley).

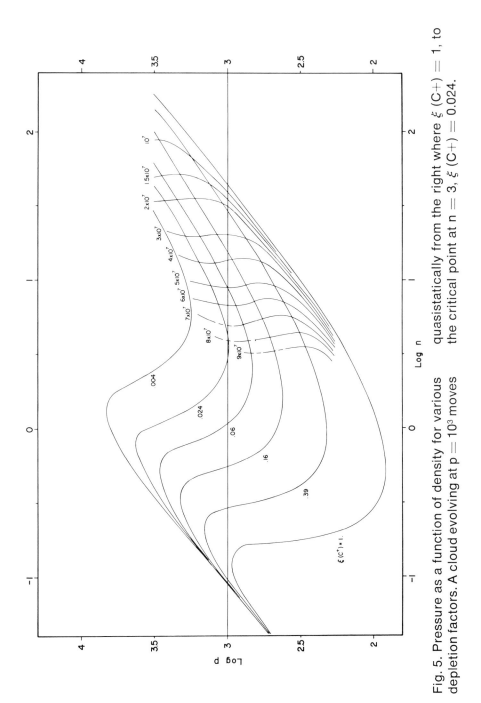

Fig. 5. Pressure as a function of density for various depletion factors. A cloud evolving at $p = 10^3$ moves quasistatically from the right where $\xi\,(C+) = 1$, to the critical point at $n = 3$, $\xi\,(C+) = 0.024$.

It is believed (but has not been proved) that at this point the evolution of a small cloud will proceed at constant pressure, but on the faster thermal time scale of 10^{6-7} years, with little additional depletion. This will carry the cloud to the stable point on the curve $L = 0$ at $n = 10^{-1} cm^{-3}$, $p = 10^3 cm^{-3} °K$, so that the cloud will have evaporated and again become part of the intercloud medium.

In Figure 6 we see how various quantities change with time in a cloud evolving with fixed pressure $= 10^3 cm^{-3} °K$. It moves from $n = 48$ cm^{-3}, $T = 21°K$ to $n = 3$ cm^{-3}, $T = 330°K$ in $8 \times 10^7 y$. Note the rapid decrease of Ca^{++}, as well as the slow increase in grain radius as an ice

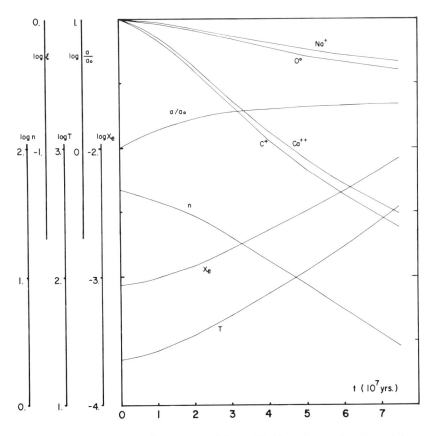

Fig. 6. Variation of various quantities with time in a cloud evolving at $p = 10^3$. Note the rapid drop in Ca^{++} compared to Na^+, and the gradual warming and expansion of the cloud.

mantle is accreted. If the ages of clouds near the sun are randomly distributed between 0 and 8×10^7 years, an age of 5×10^7 years may be typical. The properties of such a cloud would be: $n_H = 9$ cm^{-3}; $T = 100°$ K; $n_e = 0.03$ cm^{-3}; $\xi(Na^+) = 0.58$; $\xi(Ca^{++}) = 0.08$; and $\xi(Ca^{++})/\xi(Na^+) = 0.14_\odot$ which agree qualitatively with observation. Observational estimates of $\xi(Na^+)$, $\xi(Ca^{++})$, and $\xi(Ca^{++})/\xi(Na^+)$ are smaller, however, being 0.14, 0.004, and 0.03, respectively (Goldsmith, Habing, and Field, 1969). The present picture is oversimplified of course. In reality cloud collisions periodically increase the cloud pressure by factors up to 100 for short times. During such a collision, we expect that in the region immediately following the shock a variety of mechanisms will destroy the grain mantles and return the heavy atoms to the gas, including grain-grain collisions (Oort and van de Hulst) and sputtering by hot atoms (Aannestad, 1970). In the cooling region further behind the shock, the mantles will rapidly build up again because of the high density. Without the results of detailed calculations now in progress, it is difficult to see which effects will be more important and therefore whether the net effect of cloud collisions is to increase or decrease the depletion rate. We note that, as Dr. Gaustad has explained, the existence of ice mantles has been cast into doubt by infrared observations and perhaps also by the UV observations described here by Dr. Code. Therefore one should be skeptical of any model which predicts accretion of oxygen. Since sputtering of ice mantles is an attractive method of producing the water vapor observed in the gas phase (Cheung, Rank, Townes, Thornton, and Welch, 1969), perhaps oxygen is depleted under special circumstances.

We now turn to the relation between cloud models and galactic phenomena on a larger scale (Pikel'ner 1968). Much depends on one's conception of a spiral arm. Here I adopt the density-wave picture for definiteness, and first focus attention on the interarm region. According to a recent calculation of the response of the gas as it flows through the spiral pattern (Roberts, 1969), the interarm density is much lower than that in the arms as a consequence of the difference in gravitational potential (Fig. 7). This suggests that the interarm pressure is below the critical value ($p_{max} \simeq 10^3$cm^{-3}°K, depending on depletion factor) above which clouds must form. This would explain in a natural way why young stars are not found in the interarm regions, because star formation requires high density and therefore clouds. The calculations of Parker (1966) indicate that if the interarm gas is in the hot phase, it is nevertheless unstable toward the formation of magnetic wells. For adopted parameters of $n_H = 0.1$ cm^{-3}, $B = 3\mu$G, and a cosmic-ray density equal to that near the sun, the minimum e-folding time of the instability is 10^7 y, at a wavelength of 500 pc. Since this time is much shorter than the time spent in the interarm region ($\simeq 10^8$ y) the instability should be well developed, and magnetic wells separated by $\sim$ 500 pc should be common. However, if the pressure is below p_{max}, the gas may remain in the hot phase, so the scale height in the wells would be $\sim$ 100 pc. Such configurations are not clouds, but may provide the conditions for cloud formation, as explained below.

As the gas enters the gravitational field of the spiral arm, a shock forms which increases the pressure by a large factor (10 in the calculations alluded to above, which are based on a velocity dispersion of 10 km/sec in the gas, a value which happens to be appropriate for the hot gas). This increase in pressure above p_{max} forces clouds to form. Naturally they will

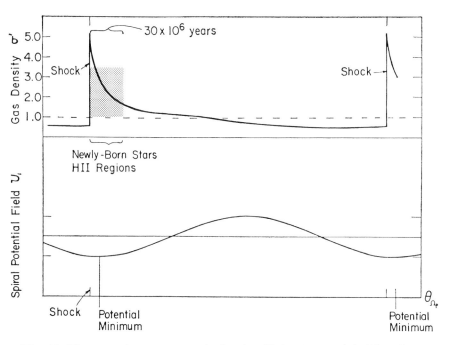

Fig. 7. The arm-interarm cycle in the Roberts model. The time between passages through the spiral arm is 2×10^8 years, roughly half in the arm and half in the interarm region. A shock occurs as the gas enters the potential well caused by the spiral arm, and the pressure increases a factor 10. This may cause the formation of clouds, particularly in magnetic wells.

form first in the magnetic wells where the pressure is highest, but if the pressure increase is large enough, they may form higher on the field lines as well. Because the cloud gas lacks buoyancy, the clouds will run down the field into the magnetic wells, and in some cases, may form new wells of their own. This is suggested by the spacing of clouds in the arm, only 100 pc. The time scale for this process is a few times 10^7 years, the cooling time for the hot gas. The process is reminiscent of "coronal rain," observed in the solar corona.

As the gas gathers into clouds, the depletion process described above commences, the zero of time in Figure 6 being that of the formation of the cloud. In about 10^8 years, a small cloud reaches the critical point and again merges with the intercloud medium if nothing intervenes to stop the depletion process. We have already mentioned the possible role of cloud collisions in this respect, but such collisions have other effects as well.

As the energy of a cloud collision is mostly dissipated into heat, colliding clouds coalesce and become more massive. In this way, a spectrum of cloud masses is established [which in a simple model (Field and Saslaw, 1965; Field and Hutchins, 1968; Penston, Munday, Strickland, and Penston, 1969) is of the form $M^{-3/2}$], in which very massive clouds are sometimes formed by the collision process. The magnetic field is decisive in opposing gravitational collapse, even of massive clouds, but if $M > 10^3 M_\odot$, the cloud collapses in about 10^7 y (if $B = 3\mu G$) (Field, 1969). Such collapses result in star formation, HII regions, supernovae II, and the other phenomena of population I. This activity has profound effects upon the gas in the spiral arm. For example, HI clouds near expanding HII regions or supernovae are accelerated outward, colliding with more distant clouds and maintaining the observed cloud motions. Grains within those particular clouds which are actually overrun by HII regions, are subjected to radiation and proton bombardment with consequent sputtering of mantle material and return of heavy elements to the gas. As the time scale for this process may be $\sim 10^8$ years, it may compete with the slow depletion considered above. Evidence that this process actually occurs is found in the more normal Ca/Na ratios in fast-moving clouds (Routly and Spitzer, 1952).

In summary, clouds form a few times 10^7 years after the shock front passes, primarily in the magnetic wells, but sometimes higher on the magnetic lines of force. In the latter case they run down along the field into the wells, colliding as they go and forming massive clouds. On a time scale of 10^8 years, heavy elements are accreted on to grains, causing them to grow a factor ~ 2 in radius and causing the depletion of heavy elements which is observed. Cloud collisions may either accelerate or retard this process, and encounters with HII regions may retard it significantly.

Clouds tend to evaporate at the trailing edge of the arm because of two factors: (i) the general reduction of pressure below p_{min} (Fig. 7), (ii) the approach of individual clouds to p_{min} because of depletion (if not retarded by other processes). Both processes occur with a time scale about 10^8 years, so it is not clear which is most important. However, we see that if depletion is not significantly retarded by cloud collisions, the lifetime of a cloud is limited to about 10^8 years. Star formation must occur on a shorter time scale if it is to succeed at all. This does not seem unreasonable if the required massive clouds accumulate by collisions occurring every 10^7 years.

We conclude with a summary of possible observational consequences of the picture described here:

(i) The boundaries of dust clouds will have thicknesses of ~ 0.04 pc, if they coincide with gas clouds.

(ii) The radii of dust grains will increase (perhaps by a factor of 2) as one goes from the shock front into the spiral arm.

(iii) Concomitantly, Ca/Na will decrease, and the clouds will on the average be warmer and less dense.

(iv) There may be a systematic velocity of clouds toward the plane as newly formed clouds move down the field lines.

(v) Some clouds will be very dense and flattened (probably with minor axes along B) as a result of cloud collisions (primarily along B).

(vi) The lower edges of dust clouds will lie along B. Hence polarization vectors will be normal to these edges.

*　　*　　*

It is a pleasure to acknowledge conversations with H. J. Habing, P. Aannestad, and P. Meszaros, as well as support by the National Science Foundation.

Discussion

Bart Bok: What you have described is Roberts' picture, basically. The thing that worries me is that I have never seen positive evidence of a higher gas density ridge. Would you not expect that in the spiral arms the 21-cm data should give evidence of a higher density as one passes through the shock? Observationally, one generally sees features that seem fairly smooth. It would be wonderful if one could really *see* a shock in the 21-cm data; but I have not seen in the data of either Harold Weaver or Frank Kerr that there is an indication of an increase in density along a ridge.

Field: I can't really comment on that except to point out that theoretically one predicts a sharp front because one is dealing with a perfect mathematical configuration for the arms and therefore the shock always occurs at exactly the same place as a function of azimuth around the galaxy. In practice, I guess we would expect this shock front to be a very wiggly thing.

Bok: Cloudiness and clumpiness come in, too. Of course, there is a star-birth ridge, but it is about 100 parsecs wide and not sharp and narrow.

Field: Right; I just can't resolve this.

G. Burbidge: What degree of compression do you expect to find in magnetic fields in these denser regions?

Field: Not very much, because it turns out that the magnetic pressure is comparable to the thermal pressure. Therefore, the pressure forces which are involved here are unable to compress the gas across the field very much. But if one exceeds a certain critical mass, calculated to be about 1000 solar masses, self-gravitation becomes important and can compress the gas across the field, increasing the field strength. So, if you have a small cloud, you do not have much compression. If you have a large cloud, you expect very significant compression of the field.

Burbidge: Can you explain the observations of Verschuur?

Field: Yes, qualitatively. There is a good correlation between the column density in the clouds which show the Zeeman effect and the magnitude of the Zeeman effect, in just the sense that one would expect. The clouds of larger column density appear to have larger fields.

C. Townes: How much confidence do you feel in the description of the shock fronts, and that there is not perhaps some finer scale instability which naturally sets in and destroys these systematic motions?

Field: Not at all confident. The search for instabilities goes on. There are three basic instabilities that have been investigated: a magneti-gravitational one which leads to the formation of wells; a thermal instability which leads to clumpiness along the lines of force; and, of course, the Jeans instability which causes contraction across the lines of force. But no doubt there are others to be found.

Townes: This is quite typical of such complex systems. It is difficult to run down all possible instabilities which may substantially change the development of the system.

Field: My philosophy is that we should try to develop conceptual pictures based on what theoretical insight we can muster, check these against observations, find out why they are wrong (and they usually are), and then proceed to the next step.

Townes: My next question is connected with the temperature history. Your discussion reminds me of the difference in temperature one finds when using ortho- and para-ammonia (and which will presumably be found in other cases). They allow us a view of the temperature history and in most cases indicate that the cloud is cooling off. For example, the clouds we have looked at seem to have been cooling off a few tens of degrees per million years. I wonder if there might be some correlation with your systematic description. For example, if there is a more gradual cooling than heating, then we have a higher probability of finding that particular thermal history rather than a past history of cooler temperatures. In any case, certain levels in the ammonia spectrum come to thermal equilibrium in a few years, and others in about one million years, and it seems that these two different relaxation times in the thermometers provided by relative populations in different molecular states might be useful in examining the long-term thermal behavior.

Field: Extremely so. In fact, in the low density phase, the cooling times are 10^7 years; in the high density phase, about 10^5 years. If you have molecular levels which relax on comparable time scales, that should be extremely interesting.

L. Aller: There is a fact that in the plasmas of gaseous nebulae we have extreme inhomogenieties that occur on very small scales — much smaller than we would have expected. As spectroscopic diagnostics are improved, additional forbidden line ratios show this; you find that these effects are more prominent than expected. There seems to be a tendency even in hot regions for nature to favor density inhomogenieties and perhaps temperature inhomogenieties as well.

Field: I want to clarify that in the picture presented in my talk, even the hot material is still HI, that is, it is still 90 percent neutral, because it is being ionized by cosmic rays rather than by ultraviolet radiation. Second, there have been a number of studies to see whether one can explain these inhomogenieties that you see in HII regions by a similar kind of process — that is, essentially a thermal instability. As you know, the situation is somewhat controversial in that some authors think thermal instabilities do occur in HII regions, while others do not.

REFERENCES

Aannestad, P. A. 1970, private communication.
Cheung, A. C., Rank, D. M., Townes, C. H., Thornton, D. D., and Welch, W. J. 1969, *Nature* 221: 626.
Clark, B. G. 1965, *Ap. J.* 142: 1398.
Field, G. B. 1965, *Ap. J.* 142: 531.
————. 1969, Proceedings of 16th International Astrophysical Symposium, Liege, June 1969.
Field, G. B., Goldsmith, D. W., and Habing, H. J. 1969, *Ap. J.* 155: L149.
Field, G. B. and Hutchins, J. 1968, *Ap. J.* 153: 737.

Field, G. B., and Saslaw, W. C. 1965, *Ap. J.*: 142: 568.

Goldsmith, D. W., Habing, H. J., and Field, G. B. 1969, *Ap. J.* 158: 173.

Hjellming, R. M., Gordon, C. P., and Gordon, K. J. 1969, *Astron. and Astrophys.* 2: 202.

Kahn, F. D., and Dyson, J. E. 1965, *Ann. Rev. Astron. and Astrophys.* 3: 47.

Mebold, U. 1969, *Beitr. z. Radioastron.* 1:97.

Oort, J. H., and van de Hulst, H. C. 1946, *B.A.N.* 10: 187.

Parker, E. N. 1966, *Ap. J.* 145: 811.

Penston, M. V., and Brown, F. E. 1970, *M. N.* 150: 373.

Penston, M. V., Munday, V. A., Stickland, D. J., and Penston, M. J. 1969, *M. N.* 142: 355.

Pikel'ner, S. B. 1968, *Sov. Astron. — A. J.* 11: 737.

Radhakrishnan, V., and Murray, J. D. 1969, *Proc. Astron. Soc. Australia* 1: 215.

Roberts, W. W. 1969, *Ap. J.* 158: 123.

Routly, P. M., and Spitzer, L., Jr. 1952, *Ap. J.* 115: 227.

Silk, J., and Werner, M. W. 1969, *Ap. J.* 158: 185.

Spitzer, L., Jr. 1951, *Problems of Cosmical Aerodynamics,* Proc. of I.A.U. Symposium in Paris, 1949 (Dayton, Ohio, Central Air Documents Office), Ch. 3, p. 31.

—————. 1968, *Diffuse Matter in Space* (New York: Interscience), p. 181.

Spitzer, L., Jr., and Scott, E. H. 1969, *Ap. J.* 158: 161.

Stone, M. E. 1970, *Ap. J.* 159: 277 & 293.

13. In Retrospect

LEO GOLDBERG

Harvard College Observatory

The valuable information assembled in this volume certainly in itself pays fitting tribute to Bart J. Bok, but most of us involved in this Symposium also know him as an inspirational teacher and friend, whose personal warmth and enthusiasm as much as the bare subject matter, made astronomy seem so attractive as a career. There would be much less discontent among students today if there were more professors like Bok on university campuses.

Taking a course from him was a unique experience. I have never seen any other teacher who was able to explain Kepler's Laws while simultaneously acting out the parts of the sun, the moon, and the earth.

One of his best-known pedagogic inventions was the star-counting circuit. It was not an electronic device, but a network of midwestern and southern colleges and universities at which he placed his former students, each with responsibility for a section of the Milky Way.

Dr. McCuskey has described this early star count program and its results. The original purpose of the program was to delineate the galactic structure out to modest distances from the sun. Most of the early work consisted of general star counts, but the investigation of stellar distribution is much more effective when the counts are made with stars grouped into narrow intervals of spectral type and luminosity. Studies of this kind have been made possible by the advent of wide field telescopes equipped with objective prisms, and the astronomers at the Stockholm and Warner and Swasey observatories have been most active in this field of investigation.

Star counts were originally intended as a means of determining the distribution of stars in space, in the hope that they might eventually reveal a spiral arm in the solar neighborhood. As we know, other methods have proven to be more powerful, for example, Baade's work on the Andromeda Nebula has shown that OB stars and diffuse nebulae can be used as tracers for spiral structure and, of course, the 21-cm measurements are even more effective for this purpose. One outcome of the investigation of spiral arms in the galaxy was the recognition that young stars are associated with gas and dust, and therefore that stars are probably formed from dust. This discovery attached enormous importance to studies of the sizes, the structures, the dynamics, and the composition of dust clouds, studies in which star counts have played a vital role.

In recent years, Bok and his collaborators in Australia and the United States have concentrated on studies of the sizes, the masses, and the absorbing properties of dust clouds by refined methods of star counting in which accurate spectral or multicolor photometry is applied to large numbers of stars in the neighborhoods of dust clouds. John Graham showed us how powerful this technique is as a means of discovering clouds in the Carina region; in particular the Chilean studies have led to the discovery of a dark cloud in front of and much closer to the earth than Carina (at a distance of about 1 kiloparsec). The determination of color excesses by precise photoelectric techniques was described by David Crawford; the accuracy of these measurements is such that fluctuations of a few thousandths of a magnitude from star to star are significant.

Dr. Elvius explained how the sizes, shapes, and compositions of the interstellar grains can also be studied by observing the polarization of starlight passing through clouds of aligned, asymmetric dust grains, an effect first discovered independently by Hiltner and Hall in 1949. Dr. Elvius showed us how measurements of polarization at different wavelengths can give information on the size distribution of grains around the star Merope in the Pleiades. The chemical composition of these grains is not clearly established, although silicate grains with impurities seem the most likely candidates. Graphite grains and ice-coated graphite grains now seem to be ruled out because Purcell has recently shown that their diamagnetism makes it difficult to align the particles in a magnetic field.

Bok, in his own work, has pioneered in the study of the so-called globules, which are the smallest known dark nebulae. Their importance as protostars was first pointed out by Bok and Reilly in connection with M8 in 1947. Bok described current work here at the University of Arizona in which he, in collaboration with Miss Cordwell, and Dr. Cromwell, have used the 90-inch telescope and a Carnegie image tube to photograph a selection of well-delineated globules. These dense clouds of interstellar grains are very cold; the temperatures may be as low as 7 degrees absolute. The small ones have diameters of 10,000 astronomical units and masses about half that of the sun. The larger ones have diameters of up to 100,000 astronomical units and masses about 35 times that of the sun. The Arizona group has also discovered larger cool clouds; one of these has a diameter of 12 light years and a mass of over 2,000 suns. It is now suspected that small globules collapse into single stars in a few million years, while large globules may end up as massive single stars or as star clusters.

In 1951 Ewen and Purcell at Harvard discovered the 21-centimeter line of neutral hydrogen in the galaxy. Bart Bok was one of the first astronomers in the United States to undertake systematic observations of this line, first with a 24-foot telescope and later with a 60-foot dish. At that time radio astronomy research was almost absent at universities in this country, Cornell and Ohio State being notable exceptions. Bok initiated the training of radio astronomers at Harvard and his early students in that period included Dieter, Drake, Heeschen, Kassim, Lawrence, Lilley, Menon, Varsavsky, and Wade. Mention of these names serves to illustrate how much the early development of radio astronomy in this country owes to his efforts. As described by Menon, much of the work of that group was devoted to studying the ratio between gas and dust in neutral clouds. At present it seems to be well established that there is a definite decrease in 21-centimeter emission from dark regions but that this decrease might be caused either by the depletion of hydrogen as a consequence of molecule formation or by lower temperatures. The matter is still not entirely settled.

Dr. Dieter reviewed the recent astonishing discoveries of radio spectral lines. Through the 1950s and the early 1960s, only one spectral line — at 21 centimeters — was known in radio astronomy. In the last few years spectral line radio astronomy has burgeoned with the discovery of hydrogen recombination lines, molecular OH, ammonia, water, and formaldehyde, and isotopes containing C^{13} and O^{18}. Spectacular maser effects were discovered in OH and H_2O resulting from overpopulation of upper levels and the inverse "daser" effect caused by the overpopulation of the lower level in formaldehyde. These new observations put very severe constraints on cloud models, as Dr. Dieter illustrated. Not mentioned is the emission of radio lines of carbon which probably originate in H I regions; we hope shortly to be observing hydrogen lines from H I clouds as a result of recombination emission by the very tiny amount of hydrogen which is ionized by cosmic rays and X-rays. Dr. Gaustad described his work on the composition of interstellar dust, which is very important because of the role played by dust in the formation of molecules and in determining the heat balance of a protostar in the early stages of gravitational collapse. Dr. Gaustad explained why the composition of dust is best studied in the infrared part of the spectrum where the fundamental vibration-rotation bands of molecules lie. These bands retain their identity in solids whereas electronic bands are completely changed in the solid state. No ice has yet been found in the spectra of reddened stars, but there is evidence for silicate absorption. The beautiful measurements of extinction with the OAO, as reported by Code suggest that a mixture of silicates and graphite and other solid particles could account for the average observed extinction curve in the ultraviolet, visible and infrared.

The observational properties of what may be newly forming stars, such as T Tauri, the Orion population-type stars, and flare stars were described by Dr. Kuhi who concluded that low mass stars do form in dark clouds, but it is not clear whether OB stars are needed to stimulate or catalyze the process. The infrared measurements of Dr. Low show that in most infrared sources (except for the galactic center and other galactic nuclei), radiation is produced by thermal reradiation by dust of the ultraviolet radiation it absorbs from hot stars. In the case of newly forming stars, the dust is located in rapidly-expanding outer shells, and Dr. Low has shown how the physical properties of these objects can be inferred from the spectral measurements in the visible and in the infrared. One of the problems is that the observed infrared flux is so large that ordinary gravitational contraction seems unable to account for it unless the masses are very high or (as Dr. Townes pointed out in the discussion) the lifetime of the high flux is short.

Finally, Dr. Field considered the formation, history and longevity of clouds. The sizes and densities of the clouds are such that they are not bound gravitationally and internal pressure would make them expand and dissipate in about 10 million years. He discussed three possibilities for confining the gas and clouds: one is dynamic pressure, by the impact of other clouds; another is magnetic stress; and the third is gas pressure in an external medium of low density. Calculations based on the third possibility suggest that interstellar gas, when heated by cosmic rays and X-rays and cooled by the radiation of forbidden lines excited by electron collision, can exist in pressure equilibrium in two stable phases. In one phase, which corresponds to the intercloud medium, the density is low and the temperature high; in the other, the clouds, high density goes with low temperature. Very important is the extent to which the interstellar atoms and ions are "locked up" in the grains and thus inhibited from acting as cooling agents. Field shows how atoms and ions may be accreted by the grains and knocked off in collisions between clouds. The problem is as fascinating as it is difficult to solve. The study of physical processes in dark clouds is evidently in its very early stages.